Dedicated to Ma

GU01086826

'When the well is dry, they k

We cannot, in this age of clean and plentiful water pipes houses, appreciate the problems arising from having to rely on wells and springs. They were often unreliable, could become undrinkable, dried up in summer and froze in winter.

In spite of all these problems, our ancestors had to fetch all the water they needed for cooking, washing, bathing, laundry, and drinking. Often a considerable distance had to be covered, usually on foot to collect the daily needs. This situation was common within living memory and exists occasionally today in remoter areas.

Many of these supplies survive, springs more than wells for the latter are easily lost. Derbyshire has a rich and much neglected heritage of springs and wells. There is nowhere in Britain where such a variety of types of well and spring can be found within a small area; petrifying wells, ebbing and flowing wells, thermal springs, Holy wells, spa waters and the tradition of well dressing.

Grid references are given only for sites that can be visited with ease. These are given as six figure references within the Ordnance Survey square SK on sheet numbers 119, 120, 128, and 129 in the new 1:50000 series. The 1:25000 Outdoor Leisure Maps, 'The Dark Peak' and 'The White Peak' are especially useful for they feature many wells and springs in blue, and some are named.

Units in common useage are used throughout in imperial measure and equivalent metric measure. One rare and disused measure is the hogshead which has been converted on the basis of one hogshead being equal to 63 gallons (286 litres). References will also be found to g.p.d. and m.g.d. being abbreviations for gallons per day and millions of gallons per day. These are common units in the water supply industry and in each case the day is a full one of 24 hours.

'Ancient Wells and Springs of Derbyshire'
Phototypesetting and artwork by Prior to Print, 44 Friar Gate, Derby
Printed by the Heanor Gate Printing Company, Heanor, Derbyshire

© Peter Naylor 1983

No part of this book may be reproduced in any form or by any means
without the permission of the Owner of the Copyright

Published by **Scarthin Books**, Cromford, Derbyshire
ISBN 0 907758 010

Town Well ('Etta's Well') at Etwall

Ancient Wells and Springs of Derbyshire

by Peter J. Naylor

Photography by David Mitchell

Scarthin Books, Cromford 1983

Contents

CHAPTER ONE

INTRODUCTION

Why they are where they are

Rainwater is the source of all our water. It supplies our streams, which become rivers which feed the seas. All rivers start as springs and further springs add to them, either directly or through other streams and rivers. Evaporation of the sea water creates vapour in the form of clouds, which condense over the land mass as rain or snow. It is a perpetual cycle and the fertility of a country is gauged by its rainfall.

The rain soaks into the earth and filters through the various strata until it meets an impervious layer. There the water will form a level, known as the water table, and will run off either below ground, or to the surface where the impervious layer outcrops. Springs therefore appear at the surface wherever the upper face of an impervious layer outcrops. A well is sunk into the water table where springs are not available.

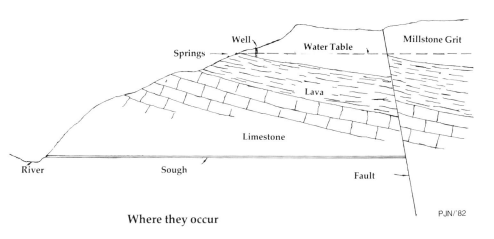

Where they occur

The Derbyshire dome is of limestone, capped on its margins by millstone grit, a form of sandstone. The two are separated by a band of shale. There are strata of volcanic lava in the limestone. The shale and lava (toadstone) are impervious and where these outcrop are found numerous springs characteristic of the area. The limestone dome is dry in spite of the heavy rainfall, due to the mineral veins and

5

Wormhill Springs, feeding the Wye in Chee Dale

fissures which are vertical or nearly so, and which act as drains. The activities of the lead miner with his mine shafts and soughs has further encouraged drainage in this area. There are limestone outliers at Ashover, Crich, Snelston and Ticknall with Calke.

The millstone grit in the north of the county, with its shales, forms very large catchments. This was recognised and gave the impetus to the damming of the valleys for the Derwent valley scheme of reservoirs. The catchment has an area of 23000 acres (9300 hectares) and supplies Derby, Nottingham and Leicester. A visit to these dams is well worth while, for they are most attractive and somewhat reminiscent of Scottish lochs.

The coal measures in the Nottinghamshire/Derbyshire border and the Leicestershire/Derbyshire border are a rich source of water suitable for wells and springs. The presence of coal mining and the consequent increase in population has caused widespread pollution of these sources. However, many of the towns drew their water from colliery shafts until recent times.

The bunter sandstone and keuper marl, in the south of the county are ideal for wells and boreholes with few springs. The alluvial valleys of the Trent and lower Dove can support wells only.

Some would boast that the best water comes from the bunter. Different areas have different claims that 'their water' is the best. Tastes differ and generally one's taste favours the familiar. There is little doubt that the naturally occuring waters in Derbyshire are mostly very pure and pleasant to drink

A borehole at Ashbourne is the source of the 'Ashbourne Water', one of only three natural waters in Britain to be bottled and sold commercially, Buxton water is also bottled and sold. The Nestlé Company searched the country for a suitable water and finally settled for one of their own supplies, at the milk condensery at Ashbourne, where they have four boreholes and one of these is used. They launched the bottled water in 1976 as a limited trial. In the space of five years they had captured 30% of the United Kingdom market of forty million litres (nearly nine million gallons) per year, with anticipated sales of £27-£28 million pounds a year. It is of interest to note that there are over forty different brands of bottled water available in the United Kingdom. An artesian well (named after Artois in France) is a borehole wherein the water pressure is so great that it rises to the

Filter jars by Pearson and Co. (Chesterfield)

Ashbourne Water label; Nestlé Co.

photo. the author

7

surface without the aid of pumping. The author could not find such an artesian well in the county. An artesian, 393 feet (120m) deep and sunk in London in 1844 supplies the fountains in Trafalgar Square.

The contamination of the water supplies was an ever increasing problem, due mostly to the pollution caused by industrial development and over-population in the early part of the last century. A brisk trade started at this time in water purifiers. These were made by the stoneware potteries, especially those in the Chesterfield area. They were filter jars using charcoal and sand as media. Water was poured into the top which had a lid, and was drawn off through a tap at the bottom. A particularly good filter jar was made by Oldfield and Company at the Welshpool and Payne Potteries from 1823 onwards.

Some of these were very ornamental, having white decorations in relief on a cream coloured jar. The pottery would inscribe any name and description on the jar as chosen by the purchaser. Thus a Derbyshire filter jar would appear in London as 'The Atkins Filter' supplied by the Engineering and Water Softening Co., London. These were strictly filters, not softeners. They did not eliminate bacterial infection, as some people thought. Oldfields, along with several other potteries near Chesterfield were taken over by James Pearson Ltd., now Pearson and Co. (Chesterfield) Ltd., who have a well at their Pottery Lane, Whittington Moor premises. This is brick lined, 18 feet (5.5m) deep, 4 feet (1.2m) in diameter. The water lies on the coal measures and the water, two million gallons (nine million litres) per annum is mixed with the clay. (SK.386734).

Place Names

There are numerous place names in Derbyshire indicative of wells and springs. These usually refer to a spring, from the Old English 'wella', 'waella' or 'waelle', which sometimes means 'well' or 'stream'. The first half of such place names often refer to a personal name; Bakewell (Badeca's spring), Glapwell (Glappa's spring), Wigwell (Wicga's spring), Tideswell (Tidi's well), etc.

Other names refer to the nature of the water; Blackwell (dark spring, black and blake were synonymous, as in Blake Mere), Whitwell (clear spring), Caldwell (cold spring). In some instances the references are to streams; Bradwell (broad stream), Hopwell (stream in a branch valley), Etwall (Eata's stream). There are some place names where the well element has become disguised as in Dowel, Acre Wall, and Hargatewall. There is one extraordinary place name, Daniel Hay in the parish of Smisby. This name means spring of the Danes (Dene, waella). Hay is an enclosure. A spring can be seen close to Daniel Hay Farm (SK.344207).

Thoroughfares carrying the name well are common; in Chesterfield there are Beetwell Street (after the Bete family), Dowdeswell Lane and Holywell Street. There is Coldwell Street in Wirksworth and a Coldwell End in Youlgreave. Becketwell Street in Derby along with Well Street and Spa Lane are other examples.

One notable exception is Whatstandwell, named after a Walter Stonewell who lived close by, but where did he get his name?

Making a Spring or Well

Springs are self evident. They burst to the surface as if by a miracle and either run to or create a stream, or soak away. A good and reliable spring was often the pre-requisite for the siting of an early settlement. The importance of a reliable source of clean water to a community is obvious. What is not so obvious is the necessity to have it close to, or within the community. Before pipes were rendered easy to make and simple to lay, and before the invention of small but efficient pumps, water had to be carried; a difficult and heavy task. It must be remembered that until recently streams were clean enough to be usable as drinking water. Springs are commonplace in the hilly areas of the county. If they were used frequently the ground quickly became muddy, which in turn made the water dirty. The local inhabitants would pave the area surrounding the spring, often placing an arch over the point of issue to protect it from cattle. Some were fenced, and a stone trough frequently employed as a pail dip. In the lower parts of the county, particularly in the Trent and Dove plains, wells had to be sunk to the water table.

The decision on where to sink was based on either local knowledge, the lie of the land, previous experience and guessing, or a dowser (water diviner) was employed. A good dowser was often in demand, and he (very rarely she) could not only determine the place to dig but would give an estimate of the depth necessary to dig, often with an accuracy within ten per cent.

The well sinker would then start his work. It was a slow and laborious process and was often dangerous. He would dig a vertical shaft, similar to a mine shaft but smaller. He would be on his own, there was insufficient space for two. It certainly required courage. A helper or helpers would station themselves at the top of the shaft where a windlass would be erected. The upper part of the well would be through soft ground and it would be necessary to line this section with bricks or dressed stone. An overlarge shaft would be dug into which would be placed a support ring or collar. This was usually timber; the better ones being shod with iron.

A lining or steening (steining, steynin) would be built on to this collar. By excavating the shaft, the collar would sink slowly with the steining. The well sinker would send the dirt up to the surface, a bucketfull at a time, bricks or stones would be sent down in the returning bucket. The lead miners in the Peak District lined their mine shafts with dry stone walling known as ginging (the first g is hard, the second soft) and the bucket used was known as a kibble. This expertise in sinking mine shafts was often used for sinking well shafts. As soon as rock or hard clay was reached, the lining would cease. The sinker would continue until a permanent level of water was reached, always on the upperside of an impervious layer such as heavy clay, coal, shale or toadstone.

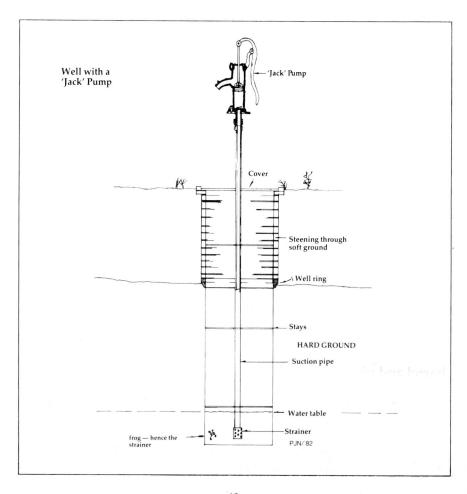

Well with a 'Jack' Pump

'Jack' Pump

Cover

Steening through soft ground

Well ring

Stays

HARD GROUND

Suction pipe

Water table

frog — hence the strainer

Strainer

PJN/'82

10

The end result, after a few days had elapsed to allow for the settling of mud, was either used as a well, using a windlass and pail, or in more recent times may have been fitted with a pump.

These wells were very important parts of a property, although they were often shared. So important were they, that they were written into deeds and Court Rolls. For example, the Court Roll for Ilkeston in 1877, has a reference '. . . the users in common with others entitled thereto of the well of Hard Water and Apparatus for drawing water therefrom in the Yard belonging to the Old Harrow Inn'. The apparatus would be a pump. The Old Harrow Inn was demolished in 1896.

Latterly it was commonplace to sink a well in an allotment garden. A simple substitute for steening was the use of barrels or oil drums with the ends removed. These are a hazard in disused gardens and there are frequent reports of people or animals having to be rescued from them. Repairs were often necessary, as the walls of the well might collapse and choke the shaft. Such repairs were dangerous undertakings for the operative, for he often risked being buried alive.

There is a record, just outside the county at Tutbury Castle, where the well had to be repaired in 1438. The well bottom had to be kept dry by bailing whilst the masons worked at a depth of over 120 feet (36.6m), the normal depth of water is 12 feet (3.7m) in a 5 feet (1.5m) diameter shaft. A daunting task indeed. (SK.210302).

Lifting Well Water

A shallow well presented few problems. Dipping of pails was sufficient and sometimes a hook on a stale, similar to a shepherd's crook, was used to raise and lower the container. A spring catch prevented the loss of the bucket.

The pails were made by wet coopers and had wooden hoops originally. Later they were bound with iron hoops, with rope or iron handles. Pumps were installed by those who could afford them and these were sited over the wells. Subsequently boreholes were driven for these pumps, a quicker, easier and safer device than well sinking. The first pumps had wooden barrels, plungers and pipes, the product of the village carpenter. Great skill was required for the boring of the barrel and pipes, which was done by hand using an auger. Elm was much favoured for this work. The pipes were jointed with mutton fat and lowered down the well, stays kept the pipe central in the well shaft. The plunger or bucket was of wood and incorporated a clack valve, a non-return device, made from leather. The local blacksmith provided the spout, pump rod and handle. The fitting of pumps allowed the wells to be sealed at the top on a semi-permanent basis.

This improved the cleanliness of the water supply, as it prevented animals and debris falling down the shaft. The tales of what had been found in wells are apocryphal and not for the squeamish! These pumps did not freeze in winter, but were difficult to repair. If the pipe failed, the entire assembly had to be raised.

Lead came into use early in the county, probably because it occurs naturally in the Peak District. Lead pumps with lead pipes were made for those who could afford them. They required less maintenance but froze easily. They were, therefore cased in timber. Lead gave way to cast iron at the turn of the eighteenth century, when such pumps, with wrought iron pipes became a standard product of foundries.

The writer could not find a timber pump extant anywhere. There must be a few lead ones in the county but they are difficult to find. There are numerous cast iron pumps to be found, many still in use.

As the atmosphere will only support a column of water of 34 feet (10.4m) these pumps would not work on a lift of more than 25 feet (7.6m) and 22 feet (6.7m) was normal. Greater depths required pumps at a lower levels, and occasionally a series of pumps known as 'lifts'.

Pump at Over Haddon, recently tidied up   Wood-cased pump at Hardwick Hall

A thatched pump in use; *photo. Rosa Davies, courtesy of Museum of English Rural Life*

These cast iron pipes were known as Jack Pumps, and one manufacturer featured a lion's head on the body thus lending the name 'lion pump' to these models. A lion's head featured on many spouts on pumps, springs, etc. A rotary version was made whereby a crank wheel, identical to the old mangle wheel connected to a jack pump by means of a crank. The water was caught in troughs usually cut out of a single piece of stone, but sometimes of brick or lead; hooks or stands were sometimes provided for the buckets. The luckier householders had pumps fitted in the kitchen thus saving the chore of fetching water in all weathers. The modern well user raises his water by electrically driven centrifugal pumps.

Transportation

It was not unusual for the housewives to fetch their water from the communal well or spring. At the worst it meant a lengthy walk in bad weather. At best, if you were lucky you had a private well in the back garden. The women used to congregate and enjoy a gossip on these occasions. News would be exchanged along with village tittle-tattle. It has been said that the laying of piped water supplies to the houses destroyed much of the community spirit, by rendering the fetching of water unnecessary. Where the journey was long, water would be carried in pails, one in each hand with the help of a shoulder yoke. This latter helped to prevent spillage and placed the weight onto the shoulders. The fetching of water by cart was common, some carts being specially built for the purpose, comprising a large horizontal barrel on wheels. It is still possible to see farmers fetching water from springs in churns in the county.

Some villages enjoyed piped water before the formation of the public water companies, as at Sudbury, Kedleston and Youlgreave. This was usually by courtesy of some estate or local benefactor. The water used was spring water held in a small reservoir. Where the water had to be lifted from its source to a community on higher ground a hydraulic ram was used. The ponderous beat of these was once a common sound in parts of the county.

Dewpond fed from a spring, near Friden

Other Sources

If spring or well water was not readily available, householders would collect rainwater from the house roof. We are all familiar with rainwater butts, the original ones being coopered from wood. Lately, plastic has taken over. In some areas this was the only source of water for all purposes, including drinking water, a situation that existed into this century as at Wardlow and Little Hucklow where roof water was collected in meres. The so-called dew ponds, are in effect rainwater pools, designed to collect the maximum amount of water with minimum amount of evaporative loss. These are in use throughout the county for watering cattle, particularly where the distance from springs and streams is great. They are now discouraged (or even banned) to comply with EEC regulations. The meres in the county were also for domestic purposes, relying on rainwater for replenishment.

Colour

It is interesting to compare the different colours of natural waters, by collecting them in a clearglass bottle of at least two inches diameter. They are often clear, but more frequently they are tinged with colour; blue, green or yellow with variations between these colours.

CHAPTER TWO

Holy Wells, Ancient Customs and Legends

Holy wells were an institution in this country prior to the dissolution of the monasteries. They would be much frowned on today, although many Britons travel to the continent to visit such places in much the same way that they were visited here hundreds of years ago. Tradition has it that a holy well should face the east, presumably to the Holy Land. Without doubt the most famous holy well in Derbyshire was St. Anne's Well at Buxton. This is dealt with in chapter four as its importance as a spa eventually outweighed its importance as a holy well.

St. Alkmund's Well

Alkmund the son of Alered, King of Northumbria was killed in battle by the Danes and was buried at Lilleshal in Shropshire. He was canonised as a saint and martyr for having died in defence of Christianity against the 'heathen' invaders. His body was disinterred secretly by monks and conveyed to Northworthy, the present day Derby, so as to avoid its capture by the Danes. On arrival, his corpse was laid at the side of a spring, known as St. Alkmund's Well to this day, whilst a permanent resting place was built nearby. This chapel was commenced in 820, a year after St. Alkmund's death, and

Sharder Well, Hackney, once an important water source

15

contained a shrine to the saint. St. Alkmund's Well never compared with St. Anne's Well at Buxton, but was popular with Northumbrians until the dissolution of the monasteries, when such were banned. It was said that 'north-country-men enquire of his tomb and rest their packs upon it' after the Reformation, so the tradition lived on for a time.

The well can be seen at the junction of Bath Street and Well Street, overshadowed by Derby's only tower block of flats. Water still issues from it, for it is a spring, but it is ignored and used as a repository for old bottles and other rubbish. There has been talk of renovating it and preserving this relic. The church built in 1844 on the site of the chapel was demolished in 1967 to make way for road 'improvements'. St. Alkmund's sarcophagus can be seen in Derby Museum.

Surprisingly the well does not appear on Speed's map of Derby dated 1610, at a time when it was the centre of a popular pilgrimage, but does appear on Moneypenny's map of 1791 and Brayley's map of 1806. So perhaps the well was held in higher esteem of late than one might imagine. It has been dressed from time to time this century, a custom that extended into the adjoining streets where some of the houses were decorated. These dressings took place on Ascension Day, with a notable dressing on 24th May 1945, when the theme was 'We love Him because he loved us', a celebration of the cessation of hostilities in Europe.

Kings Newton

The Holy-well or Holiwell was situated on Wards Lane, once believed to have been the packhorse route from Derby to Swarkestone Bridge prior to the building of Cavendish Bridge at Shardlow. Many a thirsty chapman and his horses probably refreshed themselves here. The spring once sported a canopy which bore the inscription *'Fons Sacer Hic Struitor Robertus Nominis Hardinge' 16??'* or translated 'This Holy Well is constructed by Robert of the name Hardinge.' The date was effaced, one authority gives it as 1600, a guide of 1846 gives it as 1688. The portal of the arch faced due east, traditional with Holy wells, but unfortunately this was accidently demolished recently by the collapse of an adjacent ash tree. All that remains is a muddy patch, but there is a scheme afoot to dig it out and restore it, by the Melbourne Civic Society. J. J. Briggs wrote in 1852 'Probably to this spot once repaired a deluded votary to drink the supposed sacred water and in return for benefits received, to leave a votive gift'. The Packhorse Inn dated 1727 reminds us that this was once an important thoroughfare. The Hardinge family were the local Lords of the manor; the Hardinge Arms nearby commemorates this.

Chesterfield

The Holy Well at Chesterfield is remembered by Holywell Street, the earliest recorded thoroughfare in the town, referred to as Haliwellegate in a deed of 1245. The Haliwell itself is first mentioned in 1196. Holywell Street led to the well which originally was contained within the chapel dedicated to Saint Helen. This chapel used to stand in what later became the play ground of the Old Grammar School, now part of the Chesterfield College of Technology.

The dedication of the chapel to Saint Helen is of interest. The cult of Saint Helen (Ellen) is often associated with wells, for she was a saint much favoured by well worshippers. She is associated with the Celtic saint Elian, a supposed descendant of Ella, the water sprite. It is a name which is also associated with Roman settlements, as at Derby, Norwich and York. Near to the Old Grammar School is a row of terraced houses called Sunny Springs, and nearby is Dowdeswell Street, off Abercrombie Street. Chesterfield's old market pump has recently been restored by a local engineering firm. John Wesley preached from this pump when he visited Chesterfield. There is a Beetwell Street in Chesterfield, and this with Holywell Street, is a medieval road. There is also Spa Lane, but nothing is known of a spa or bath house in the area. The reference above to a 'Haliwell' is of interest for there is a place name in Matlock Dale associated with the thermal springs in 1374 of 'Haliwellker'.

Well Dressing

Derbyshire is a county especially rich in customs and without doubt one of its most beautiful customs is well dressing, which is unique to the county. Modern day well dressing is mostly a revival, and the methods used are comparatively recent. The original dressings, without doubt of Celtic origin, were simpler affairs.

Crichton Porteous, the doyen of local writers, wrote, 'How right, . . that water in this county should' have its special ceremonies, and an expert craft'.

The origin of well dressing is lost in the mists of time. The religion of the Celts, our ancestors, was a form of nature worship, stamped out by the advent of Christianity. The Peak District of Derbyshire is a stonghold of the remnants of this beautiful religion, which puts emphasis on the seasons, harvests, and other natural phenomena. In the church of St. Giles at Matlock, also at Ashford in the Water and Trusley, can be seen maidens' garlands or crantses, the pathetic reminders of the deaths of the bethrothed. The garlanding ceremony

17

St. Alkmunds's Well, Derby
before removal of one sack of rubbish
and two pence (replaced)

Table Pump to lift water to the roof
of Elvaston Castle
by Harrison of Derby, 1834

at Castleton is a strange but disturbing ceremony. In Celtic times the springs in the Peak District were probably decorated with simple posies and garlands as votive offerings to the earth Goddess. The uninterrupted supply of clean water is important to us all, and more so over two thousand years ago, when springs suffered from the vagaries of the weather.

Our ancestors certainly worshipped springs, and authority deemed it necessary to stamp it out. The Council of Arles decreed in 452 that anyone who worshipped 'trees, fountains or stones' would be found guilty of sacrilege. The Kings Edgar and Canute forbade well worship, and St. Anselm in 1102 condemned the practice in London. This is why so many wells and springs were endowed with saints' names. It enabled the populace to continue with a modified well worship under the patronage of the church. There are several springs in the area dedicated to saints; St. Anne at Buxton and Nottingham, St. Alkmund at Derby, St. Bertram near Dovedale, but in Staffordshire.

The practice of well dressing fell into disuse and was revived recently, and sometimes dressings have been inaugurated without historical precedent. The oldest surviving dressings are those held at Tissington, and to the connoisseur, they remain the best.

Today's dressings are very elaborate and have developed into a craft. These methods were introduced from 1800 onwards when the dressings were reinstituted. Instead of garlands of old, elaborate designs with texts were introduced.

Someone designs the dressings, and decides how the picture will be set out, and which materials will be used. Everyone joins in; men, women and children and at some villages there are dressings undertaken entirely by children. Competitions are held and prizes awarded for the best dressings. This ensures the maintenance of high standards of craftmanship.

The displays comprise panels of varying sizes, some as big as six feet (1.83m) high and four feet (1.22m) wide, arranged over and round a water supply. These are often in the form of a tryptich and appear to be similar to altar panels. Each panel is of wood with raised edges, into which is smoothed well-pugged clay. This clay is re-used year after year, losses being made up with new material. The clay is held on to the boards with wire netting, tacks, etc., the panels having been soaked before the clay is added. Some are left in streams for a few days. The designer, whose word is always final, marks out the designs onto the smoothed clay from its master design. This latter is kept on display in the room for reference.

The helpers then commence filling out the design with a wide variety of materials, with strong emphasis on plants and their products. Some dressers frown on the use of sea shells, stones and minerals although these latter are pertinent to the area. A wide variety of flowers are used, which are broken down, as the various components are required. Petals are used freely, particularly hydrangea and other flowers having bold or large petals. Leaves are used, together with mosses, grasses, lichens, and seeds. Rhubarb seeds are used to great effect, as is tree bark. The purists insist that a dressing is imperfect if anything other than locally grown and gathered wild flowers are used.

To keep the materials fresh in the frames, the whole dressing is wetted at intervals, and the entire exhibit has to be begun within a few days of being placed on display. This often means that the dressers work in shifts round the clock. The competition is intense when the finished panels are finally carried out of the work place, usually the village or church hall. The panels are now very heavy, and several men struggle to carry them and lift them into position.

The wells are duly blessed by the church and a carnival atmosphere pervades the air. The local voluntary organisations are paraded with bands in attendance. Bad weather can ruin any outdoor occasion but nothing suffers more than a dressing in heavy rain. The decorations are washed out with the clay and they soon begin to look forlorn; a crushing disappointment for those who have worked long and hard to create these works of art. The dressings are then judged by an expert and prizes awarded for the best dressings. There is much friendly rivalry.

The subject matter varies, but biblical texts predominate. Sometimes an anniversary is commemorated, either local or national. 1977 saw many dressings dedicated to the Royal Silver Wedding Anniversary Celebrations. A local industry, either living or dead might be the subject, or a far away cathedral, such as Lincoln or Norwich. More dressings are taking place each year, and the standards vary considerably.

Listed below are those villages where dressings are not a recent innovation or revival:

Tissington *late May, Ascension Day*

Tradition has it that the custom started during a particularly severe drought in 1615, when these wells flowed when others in the neighbourhood has dried up. There is recorded proof that such a drought did take place that year, when only three showers fell at Winster between 25th May and 4th August. One cannot imagine the disastrous consequences of this to a community in the days before reservoirs were built to sustain us through such quirks of nature and it would account for the service taking place on Ascension Day, prior to the period of drought. Some say it dates from the Black Death (Bubonic Plague) of 1348-49, when Tissington suffered only one death, the village water receiving the credit for this deliverance.

Five wells are dressed; Town Well, Hall Well, Hands Well, Coffin Well and Yew Tree Well. The Coffin Well is named after its shape and is situated in a private garden. Hands Well is named after a family who lived in a nearby farm, (not the adjoining cottage), Yew Tree Well is self explanatory. Hall Well faces the beautiful Hall, for 400 years the home of the Fitzherberts.

The dressings here were revived at the turn of the 19th century, for they were said to have started in 1802, when an old lady, Mary Twigg, placed a garland of wild flowers and a verse on the Hall Well. They certainly existed prior to this date, for they were fully described by a Nicholas Hardinge, clerk to the House of Commons in 1758. From his description, garlands were used with an inscribed tablet. The Yew

Tree Well is now piped to local houses and farms; the Hall Well still yields 0.9 l/s (12 gpm). These dressings are recognised as being amongst some of the best in the county, set in one of the most attractive villages in the area.

Wirksworth

Taps are dressed here, but they are called well dressings. They commemorate the piping of water to the town in 1827, the year when dressings were started. The number of dressings has increased over recent years and small panels are displayed in odd places, such as the churchyard railings. These tapdressings are worth a visit, the principal ones being those by the Red Lion Inn, Wheatsheaf Inn, Methodist Church and the War Memorial. The day chosen for these is the Saturday prior to Spring Bank Holiday.

Youlgreave *late June*

This village puts up a brave show, and like Wirksworth the dressings were inaugurated in 1829 to celebrate the piping of water to the village. This remains a private water supply to this day and is dealt with in Chapter Three. Originally only the tank in the village centre was dressed, but of late five or more taps are dressed on the Saturday nearest to St. John the Baptists Day. In 1929, there were two dressings, the normal one on 24th June and another in July to commemorate the centenary of the water supply.

Hand Well, Tissington; two off-duty views

21

An Edwardian view of Mompesson's Well, Eyam

Eyam *late August*

This village is famous the world over for its heroic sacrifice during the plague of 1665, a story told many times by other authors. Several wells are dressed on Plague Sunday, the last Sunday in August, as part of the celebration, having changed from the Sunday nearest to St. Helen's Day, 18th August. One of these wells has been a water supply without interruption since 1558. The custom here was revived as late as 1951, to celebrate the Festival of Britain.

Other wells are dressed at:

Buxton *St. Anne's Well,* dressed to remember the introduction of piped water, laid by the Duke of Devonshire.

Barlow *Main Well;* another dressed as a thanksgiving for an improved water supply introduced by the Duke of Rutland in 1840. Whole flowers are used and as the panels are very heavy, they are dressed in situ. This well is now the property of the dressers by special covenant.

Tideswell *Fountain Square;* The emphasis is on three dimensional representations of ecclesiastical buildings.

A list of dressings is given at the end of this chapter.

Some of these of recent inauguration have little credibility, when plastic pools and electric pumps are used and when one of them pitches its ceremony to make it first, before Tissington. Collections are made for various charities, and the rattle of collecting boxes fills the air. This is not a recent phenomenom, for a Thomas Powell wrote in 1631 that because of the profits made by collecting at holy wells, some bogus wells were created for the enrichment of rogues. With water being piped to most houses, the value of dressing wells is lost, but the tradition lives on in all its colourful splendour.

Lost Customs

The dressing of the wells has now been revived and with so many villages indulging in the practice, its future is no doubt secure. Other traditions have succumbed to modern pressures, one of them being Bottle Day. This was always associated with children and mostly with Lady Wells.

Liquorice or Spanish Root is a flavour popular with children; the traditional region for growing the plant is not too far distant at Worksop. In some villages, within living memory, the custom of mixing well or spring water with liquorice on festival days was commonplace. In the absence of liquorice crushed sweets would be used. The children would put liquorice juice in a bottle or cup, which they would fill with spring or well water. This would then be consumed throughout that day.

At Tideswell, on Easter Sunday, the liquorice was embellished with sugar or honey, and the custom was known as sugar cupping. The water was collected from the Tor Spring at the foot of the Dropping Tor, at the side of the Manchester Road close to Brook Villa at SK.144768. A similar custom occurred at Chapel en le Frith on Whit Monday, and was known as Bottle Day. The bottles were hung round the necks of the children with string.

Belper indulged in a similar practice. Bowls or mugs were used, but oatmeal and sugar were added to the water from the Lady's Well. The wells were once dressed at Belper, and on one occasion, the Sutton in Ashfield Brass Band provided the music. They must have had a good time, for on the journey home, one of the players, much the worse for drink, fell off the coach and was killed.

The children at Bradwell collected the water and drank it out of bottles without additives. This took place on Easter Sunday, and on Palm Sunday the children placed new pins in the well to ensure a pure supply, and to protect their bottles from breaking over the Easter tide.

This appears to have been a votive offering to the Lady of the Well. The bottles were strung round the necks of the children at Chapel en le Frith, and were carried around on Easter Monday, the carriers begging sugar from the village house wives.

The children of Castleton and Great Hucklow also drank the water straight from the well. The custom at Castleton was known as shak-bottle and the water from the Well of our Lady at the top of Cave Dale, was mixed with liquorice on Good Friday. The mixture was kept in a dark place until Easter Monday, when it was taken into the church and shaken during the service. SK.148824. The palm of Palm Sunday was identified with 'pussy' willows in some areas of the county. Pussy willows were set round the Silver Well at Little Hucklow on Palm Sunday by the pupils of the Sunday School. SK.187803.

Well Dressings *a chronological list*

Late May	Tissington (Ascension Day)
	Wirksworth (Saturday prior to the Bank Holiday)
	Middleton-by-Youlgreave
	Monyash
Early June	Ashford-in-the-Water (Trinity Sunday)
Late June	Bakewell
	Hope
	Litton
	Tideswell
	Youlgreave (Saturday nearest to St. John the Baptist's Day)
Mid July	Pilsley
Late July	Stoney Middleton
Early August	Bradwell
	Barlow (Wednesday following St. Lawrence's day
Late August	Eyam (last Sunday)
	Wormhill
Early September	Hartington

The dressings are still worth seeing for a few days following the day of blessing, weather and vandals permitting.

There are other dressings at Ault Hucknall, Belper, Bonsall, Buxton, Etwall, Heath, Holmewood, and Matlock, and the list grows each year. Some of the minor dressings are badly executed and the reader is encouraged to visit one of the better known ones as listed above.

Coffin Well, Tissington, 1982   Hall Well, Tissington

Hob's Hurst Houses

There are several sites in Derbyshire known as Hob's Hurst House, a name applied to ancient burial sites. They have legendary associations, usually with giants. Hob Hurst or Hob i'th'Hurst was a wood elf. One Hob's house is referred to elsewhere in association with the water supplies to Chatsworth House and gardens.

One such Hob's Hurst House, near Buxton, is a cave, wherein have been discovered Romano-British artifacts. It is also known as Thirst House Cave and is to be found in Deep Dale south of King Sterndale, close to a spring (SK.097713) whose waters will heal the complaints of those who drink them on Good Friday. This spring has this curative virtue by courtesy of Hob himself, who tradition has it, blessed the waters. This place is often confused with another Hob's Hurst House, also variously known as Hob Thirst Hole or Hob's Hurst Cave in Monsal Dale, (SK.175713) west of Monsal Head, wherein a human skeleton of early British date was found. This cave was also inhabited by a giant Hob, who wrought numerous miracles for the general benefit of the local inhabitants. The antithesis of Puck or Robin Goodfellow, his reward for such acts of kindness was a bowl of cream left on the hearth. This attractive legend was used by Milton in his 'L'Allegro'.

Hedess's Spring

In a country so rich in legend and folklore, there is none richer than that of Hulac Warren and Hedessa.

Hulac, by tradition was a leader of a race of giants who resided in Demon's Dale or Dimmingsdale, which forms part of the valley of the River Wye. This part of the dale is overlooked by a Hob's House, an ancient earth work. One wonders if Hulac is an alternative name for Hob, or if he is of the same race of giants.

Hulac, in a moment of great passion abducted a shepherdess, Hedessa, and took her to his lair. He attempted to rape her and as a punishment he was turned to stone. This stone, the Warren stone lies in the middle of the river below Hob's House, and close to the Bakewell to Buxton road the A6. Close by are several springs, one of which is thermal at 11.5°C (53°F), the same temperature as that at the Bath House in Bakewell, and the coolest of the 'thermal waters'.

A different version of the legend has it that Hedessa threw herself off the nearby tors rather than submit to Hob's carnal desires. Where she fell, a spring of pure water rose, 'Near the place where my loved one fell, a stream of pure water, pure as her own soul, gushed forth into being, and while these mountains, and these woods and valleys remain, the spirit of my Hedessa will visit these scenes, and bless with its presence the flowing of the Hedess spring', so wrote a local magistrate. Victorian melodrama at its best.

John Howe, a local poet put the legend into verse in 1816:

> 'With grief o'erpowered she instantly expires —
> the tears dissolved beneath the hill retires —
> Hence rose the Hedessa Spring'

Fair prose for an uneducated tallow chandler. The Warren Stone is at SK173703, and the springs surround it.

CHAPTER THREE

Supplies before 'the tap'

Derby

The county's earliest water supply was the Becket Well, which alas like St. Alkmund's Church, has been swept aside; the site is now partly a shopping precinct, Duckworth Square. A plaque once recorded its one time existence, but the vandals have taken even this. The adjacent Becket Well Street is the only surviving record of this well.

Contrary to popular opinion it was not named after Thomas a Becket, but after a local of that name, also remembered in nearby Becket Street. Derby did once have a link with St. Thomas. A piece of the shirt in which he was martyred was once kept in a shrine at Darley Abbey. This sacred relic was lost at the time of the dissolution of the monasteries. One writer refers to a shrine near to the Becket Well and to pilgrimages, but it is clear that he was confusing this well with the one dedicated to St. Alkmund

Becket Well is worthy of mention for it was the source of Derby's first piped water supplies. In circa 1250, water was piped from this well to a tap in St. James's Place (now forming part of St. James Street) and to a pump in the Market Place. These pipes were tree trunks, bored through, being similar to one now in Derby Museum. This latter is, however, of a much later date, but would be almost identical in appearance. The boring of such pipes was a highly skilled process, using simple augers of the period. Prior to this piped supply, one of the earliest in the country, Derby was supplied from several wells scattered about the town. As none of these were in the town centre, water carriers conveyed the water to shops, houses, inns, etc., in barrels.

This forward thinking by the council was to the fore again in 1690, when they commissioned the famous engineer George Sorocold to install a water wheel on the River Derwent. It was coupled to a pump for raising the river water to a storage cistern sited in St. Michael's Churchyard. This wheel was unique as it was designed to rise and fall with the level of the river, which prior to the building of the weirs, varied in level considerably. The same wheel was coupled to a borer for making the pipes out of the trunks of elm trees, and also drove a malt mill. From the cistern, the water was distributed to nearby Irongate and to King Street, and further distant to the Market Place and Tenant Street, Gaol Bridge at the time. So ingenious was this machine, the entire works could be 'Managed by one man'. An early case of automation?

By 1848, this scheme was inadequate for a rapidly growing population. Derby was one of the new railway towns; the industries and population were growing apace. The better-off still had their private wells — all the Georgian houses on Friargate had one each. The poor had nothing, leading to low standards of hygiene with the consequential outbreaks of disease. In common with many other growing towns at the peak of the Industrial Revolution, small water works and town wells were getting contaminated from cess pools, industrial waste and from overfilled grave yards. This latter was more common than we would have like to have believed, and was the cause of much disease and death.

In 1848, an Act of Parliament was granted to build reservoirs on Breadsall Hill Top in the adjoining parish of the same name. Water was pumped into them from the river Derwent, upstream of Derby, using two beam engines, steam driven from coal-fired boilers, and each generating 30hp (22.4kw). These engines were housed in buildings of Victorian Gothic design with a gatehouse, where lived the engine-man. It was calculated that the average consumed by each citizen was 27 gallons (128 litres) per day, seventeen gallons (77 litres) for drinking, washing, etc., and 10 gallons (45 litres) for industry.

The water supply for Derby is now in the hands of the Severn Trent Water Authority from the Derwent Valley Scheme, with laboratories now sited at the Breadsall works. The engine house can still be seen. Whilst none of the wells, pumps and supplies mentioned can be seen, it is the story of water supply typical of a growing town, especially of a town whose population grew rapidly in the 19th century.

Bakewell

The town is so named after Baedeca's Spring, and not Baden as in the German spa town, as held by some.

The well after which this market town was named is not known, the one in the Bath Gardens is a likely contender. This was known as the Great Well and references to it crop up over the years. In 1699, 1s. 6d. (7½p) was paid, 'for dressing St. Mary's and Great Wells'. Dressing here probably means cleaning up and repairing the stonework. In the same century the Court Leet dictated 'that no person shall wash any cloathes, beasts or swines meat or filthy things either at the Great Well, Cappewell or St. Mary's Well upon pains to forfeit for any so committed, 3s. 4d. (17p)'.

By the early 1800's St. Mary's Well and the Town Well had been fitted with pumps. By 1820, the town had piped water by courtesy of the Duke of Rutland's Haddon Estate, instigated by Sir Richard Arkwright, who had a mill in the town. The townspeople had to collect their water from taps scattered about the parish.

These were replaced in 1876 by a supply from a reservoir on Coombs Hill (SK.243672) fed from springs on Fallinge Edge (SK.284674). The fountain opposite the bridge on the Baslow Road – Station Road junction (SK.220687) is a memorial to this event but ironically it was connected to the original Haddon supply, known as the Wicsop supply, which was taken from seven springs in Wicsop Wood, east of Bakewell (SK.233684). The town had to wait until 1908 before this fountain was connected to the supply that it was meant to commemorate.

The Bath House in the Bath Gardens is subterranean and is accessible through a beer cellar at the British Legion Club. The bath has a vaulted ceiling and a stone floor in which there are holes through which the spring water flows. This water is chalybeate and is 11.6°C (53°F). The volume of the water is far from constant for it varies considerably, but unrelated to the amount of rainfall.

Peat Well, Bakewell Recreation Ground

The Bath House in the Bath Gardens is subterranean and is accessible through a beer cellar at the British Legion Club. The bath has a vaulted ceiling and a stone floor in which there are holes through which the spring water flows. This water is chalybeate and is 11.6°C (53°F). The volume of the water is far from constant for it varies considerably, but unrelated to the amount of rainfall.

The Bath House was built by one of the Manners family in 1697 and was renovated about 1800, with a view to making it a spa. The Bath Gardens were named the Botanical Gardens, and bore holes were driven in an attempt to improve the water supply. The whole venture was overshadowed by the popularity of Buxton, only 15 miles (24 km) away by turnpike. Its greatest claim to fame is that the building which houses the bath was once the residence of White Watson (1761-1835). He was the bath superintendent. Also, he was a superb mason specialising in statuary and monuments, and he had a fine collection of minerals and fossils which he displayed to the public. White Watson was an extraordinarily accomplished man, the author of 'The Strata of Derbyshire', published in 1811. He made sections of the local strata by using matching stone samples carefully cut and polished. Of over one hundred of these tablets produced by him only seventeen are known to have survived; five at Derby Museum, one at Manchester Museum, three at Oxford University, one at Leicester and the remainder in private hands including three at Chatsworth.

He restored the Foljambe Tomb in Bakewell church, repaired the font and painted the clock face. He made a plaque for St. George's Chapel at Windsor to commemorate King George III's recovery of 1789, made marble ornaments (his father manufactured millstones and his uncle was a founder of the Ashford Black Marble trade). His wife was related to Sir Isaac Newton. To all this he added poetry, writing, lecturing, acting as mineral agent and many other accomplishments.

There is a further chalybeate well known as Peat Well, said to be a corruption of St. Peter's Well. This spring can be seen in the recreation ground on the east side of the Matlock road at SK.293579. Here also, plans were made to exploit the spring as a spa. Although its waters, at 13.3°C (56°F) are warmer than those at the Bath House, nothing came of this venture. This spring is now used as a feeder to a childrens' paddling pool and a fountain. The mound adjacent to the pool conceals a large iron cylindrical tank which was placed in a pit with a view to increasing the flow of water. It failed.

St. Mary's Well is across the Monyash Road from the old town hall. This like the other springs, is culverted, but the site is dressed each year.

Belper

Towards the end of the last century, there were said to be over one hundred wells in Belper. Five of these were dressed from 1839, the custom quickly dying out, although there has been an attempt at reviving the custom. The well on the Fleet, known as the Manor Well, was dressed from 1960 to 1969, although there is talk of reviving it yet again. The Taylor Well in Foundry Lane was used by the Midland Railway Company for supplying their locomotives. The wells were superceded and some were used by the Belper Waterworks Company which was established in 1860. This company, which was taken over by the Urban District Council, utilised the water from the Ladywell, springs at Springwood, Bullsmoor and Belper Lane which were impounded in reservoirs. These supplies were augmented by well bores at the confluence of the Blackbrook and River Derwent and at Chapel House Farm.

The Lady Well referred to is the only one that is well documented, one source, Charles Willott writing in 1894 tells us:

'The gem of the Park is Lady Well, — a never failing spring, gushing from the hillside through a stone spout, clear as crystal, and falling into a stone trough and hence down a gully into the brook at the bottom of the ravine'.

This was before the spring was impounded. He continues by telling us that it was a place —

'where fond lovers are wont to meet at early dawn, under the trysting tree.'

Melbourne

It is generally accepted that the village derived its name from a mill which stood by a burn or stream. The Doomsday survey certainly records a mill associated with the church. Some would argue that it derived its name from Mel — sweet, or having the taste of honey, and burn — spring. This is partly supported by an old tradition that Melbourne was once known as the 'Citie of Sweete Springes'. There used to be several springs and wells in the parish, the chief of which were the Market Place Pump, Hatton's Well, Lily Pool Spring, Shaw's Spring, Club Row, Chamber's Row, and New York Pump. At about 1890 there were 175 houses sharing 142 pumps and several wells, but an enquiry revealed that in some instances from 70 to 100 families shared only one pump. Of the water sources named only two survive and one no longer disports its pump. The exotically named Lily Pool Spring on Castle Street, (SK.388255) also revelled in a more down-to-earth name — the Wash Pit. The spring once discharged a large

An old view of the Market Place, Melbourne *photo. C. Hulley,
courtesy of Derbyshire Countryside Ltd.*

quantity of water which supplied the locality, the overflow fed a wash pit where the local vegetable growers washed their produce before market. This practice continued until recent times. The water supply was greatly reduced after a gas main was repaired close by. The Town Pump was fixed to a monument, dedicated to the passing of the Reform Act in 1832. This monument was resited in Castle Square and its site in the Market Place was taken for the Jubilee Memorial of 1887. A new pump was erected and was in use until recently. This monument is now the bus shelter, erected in 1953 to commemorate the Coronation. There is no evidence of the pump.

Of the other lost sources, Hatton's Well deserves space. It stood in Blackwell Lane opposite to the church. It was one of the wells where the water was taken by the unhygienic method of dipping. A one time parish constable, George Kinsey, fell into this well late one night and was drowned. There is no record of the state of the constable, but one could assume him to have been drunk. The well was duly covered over and a pump fitted, to be called Mary Ann Ince's Pump. In the 1830's and 1840's, Mary Ann Ince was a beer house keeper in King's Newton, George Kinsey was a wool comber, the duties of a parish constable were at the time part time and voluntary. Was Mary his amour, who protected the well to prevent further mishap, or was she filled with guilt that someone should drown after imbibing at her hostelry? The records alas do not tell us.

The New York Pump, named after the area of the same name, stood in Pump Lane, now Moira Street.

Due to the inadequacies already referred to, Melbourne connected to the Long Eaton water scheme, which drew its supply from Stanton-by-Bridge. This scheme cost £40,000 in 1892. Melbourne was connected at a cost of £3024, and paid 7d (3p) per 1000 gallons (4550 litres) for 30 years. Later a borehole was sunk at Derby Hills to augment the Stanton supply. This bore is on the north west shore of Staunton Harold reservoir.

Hardwick Hall

Derbyshire is renowned for its great houses, which are visited by many thousands each year. Little thought is given to how these houses were supplied with water, for they used large quantities, for sanitation, laundry, cooking, cleaning and in the stables. The supplies laid on to houses often extended to the adjoining village, and sometimes extended as far as an entire estate.

At Hardwick Hall the stone arched canopy on the edge of the lawn to the south of the Old Hall was St. Mary's Well (SK.462635). The

Pump in the Coal Yard, Hardwick Hall *photo. the author*

canopy once supported a lead cistern which was filled by a pump. The water in this cistern then fed by gravitation to the hall, conveyed in lead pipes which fed two further cisterns in the Low Larder. An inventory of 1601 refers to these 'sesterns of lead'. The water was then carried throughout this large house by an army of servants, a laborious and tedious job. Two Victorian hand pumps remain but are now disused. One is sited in the Coal Yard, the other in Stable Yard. They are tall, made of cast iron and are cased in wood.

Bolsover Castle

The old water supply originated outside the castle walls. To the north east, on the hillside to the east of the ravine that runs by the castle wall is a Conduit House, known locally as the Cundy. A nearby through-fare is named Cundy Street. Water rises from a spring within the house, (SK.471708), built by Sir Charles Cavendish prior to 1617. A lead pipe connected this spring to the castle, terminating at the base of a shaft which it fed. Thus a well was created from a spring. The lead pipe is mostly intact and runs under the road that goes down the ravine. A portion of it was disturbed and the pipe severed during road improvements recently. The water thus introduced into the castle was raised up the well shaft, which lies in the Well House in the north corner of the Great Court, facing the Riding School. A windlass was used in its early days, but a pump was fitted later and is still extant.

There is no public access to the Well House as the timber floor is still in a poor condition.

There are four more conduit houses built on the hillside south of the castle. They are fed from a spring on Spittle Green to the south east. These houses date from about five years after the Cundy House was built. Sir William Cavendish secured a wayleave for the pipe in July, 1622. One or more of these conduit houses provided the water to nearby cottages within living memory, and one of them has been strapped and moved bodily to make room for a road improvement scheme.

The hillsides about Bolsover abound with springs, now mostly culverted. Until recently, one such spring fed troughs on Blind Lane where the coal carter's horses drank, and where the colliers filled their 'Dudley' bottles. They had a preference for this water rather than that provided at the mine. The local doctors once had this spring water conveyed to their homes by the housemaids.

In more recent times, most of the water for Bolsover was piped from springs in the tunnel and cuttings on the railway line to Scarcliffe Station. The water runs off the coal measures from the limestone above, further springs in the two ventilation shafts adding considerably to the supply. South of the tunnel is a well 39½ feet (12m) deep, with a 140 feet (42.7m) deep bore from which water was once pumped and added to the 'tunnel' supply.

The Cundy House, Bolsover

35

Chatsworth House

The water gardens belonging to the 'Palace of the Peak' are fed from the private reservoir on Gibbet Moor. This reservoir, named Swiss Lake, supplies the renowned Emperor Fountain, Cascade and Willow Tree Fountain, and is itself supplied from Umberley Sick, a spring that rises on the moor at SK.295704. This is close to a tumulus called Hob Hurst's House. A locally held belief has it that hereabouts is a lost village, near to Umberley Well (SK.288696). The house supply comes from the Emperor Spring close to the Emperor Lake. The springs that feed this lake rise on East Moor.

Elvaston Castle

The house and offices were supplied from several wells in the area of the courtyard, most of these have been filled in and cannot be found. A pump marks the position of one of the wells and this used to be used for washing the coaches. (SK.407330). A well survives in the garden of the Kennel Cottage. A small building in the grounds was used as a pump house. A water wheel drove a pump, which was used to raise water from the lake to a cistern in the roof of the house for operating a hydraulic passenger lift.

Sudbury Hall

The village of Sudbury, including the hall, the Vernon Estate, Aston, the prison and part of the parish of Marchington are supplied with water by the Sudbury Estate owned by the Lord Vernon. The water originates from springs in Sudbury Coppice and Alder Moor Wood east of Somersal Herbert. This water rises from sand and gravel and as a consequence it becomes discoloured after heavy rain. The supply network is now very old and subjected to frequent break downs, necessitating the employment of a full time plumber. The system also supplied tanks in the roof of the hall for operating a hydraulic passenger lift as at Elvaston Castle. The large lake behind the hall is fed from a separate supply.

A Private Water Supply — Youlgreave

The Severn Trent Water Authority is for most of the residents in Derbyshire the supply undertaking, which ensures that we enjoy pure clean water at our taps. Some others rely on the Yorkshire Water Authority and North West Water for this service. A few rely on private water companies and the one at Youlgreave is unique, for it belongs to the parishioners.

The village of Youlgreave has its own water company with a board of directors drawn from local residents, and they are justifiably proud of their supply. The present chairman of the company will readily assure any stranger that the water is like wine, 'when we ask for a whisky and water at the local, we throw away the whisky and drink the water'.

Before this supply was laid the water had to be carried from the River Bradford in the valley below the village, supplemented by a few unreliable springs. Softer water for laundry and washing was caught in rainwater butts. In 1829, the villagers pooled their resources and laid a pipe from the Mawstone Spring to the Bull's Head Inn, this is the event celebrated at the well dressings. The stone collecting tank in Fountain Square holding 1200 gallons (5450 litres) and measuring 9 feet (2.74m) high and the same diameter, is an ugly reminder of this supply. The tank was and still is known as the Fountain, and was looked after by an overseer, who unlocked the tap to those who had

The Fountain, a storage tank at Youlgreave

subscribed their six pence (2½p) per annum towards the costs. This must be the lowest water rate on record.

The supply deteriorated due to the rotting and collapse of the pipe, and it was decided to lay a new one, this time from a different spring in Bleakley Wood (SK.217629) near to Mawstone Spring. The cost of this was estimated as £400, a considerable sum for a small village to raise in the 1860's. Four local benefactors came to the rescue and the men in the village were required to do the digging, 'and he who could not do his share paid another man to do it for him'. On 27th July 1869, a second opening ceremony was held at the same stone tank, followed by celebrations on a grand scale. There was a public dinner for 300 persons in the new schoolroom, 400 children marched behind the Matlock Brass Band, and it all finished with a great public tea. Dressing appears to have been an annual event thereafter except for the war years, and for some years the costs were defrayed and the dressers paid by the Youlgreave Water Committee. In return the committee received the proceeds from the collections. They relinquished this responsibility when the collection fell to 60p one year.

St. Anne's Well, Buxton, from Speed's map of Derbyshire

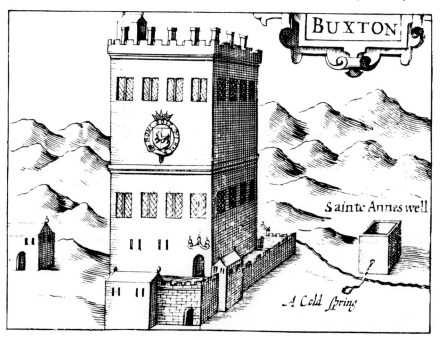

CHAPTER FOUR

Spas and Hydros or the 'Water Cure'

St. Anne's Well, Buxton

Buxton was known to the Romans, who called it Aquae Arnemetiae and used it as one of their watering places. The name suggests pre-Roman influence, for Arnemetis was a Celtic goddess. There were only two places throughout Roman Britain bearing the name Aquae, the other being Aquae Sulis, the present day Bath, in Somerset. There are both cold and thermal springs at Buxton. One of these latter was the one originally named after St. Anne, to whom the chapelry of Buxton was dedicated. By the middle of the 15th century, it was recorded as a Holy Well, and as 'principium aqua de Wye', the source of the River Wye. This is not correct for the Wye rises in the hills behind the town.

Long before this time however this well had become famous as a healing well, and was visited by thousands each year seeking relief for their ailments. At this time it would have resembled a Peakland Lourdes, with the sick and lame bathing in the water. Those who were cured left votive offerings, usually their discarded crutches, etc.

Thomas Cromwell, minister to King Henry VIII, heard of these practices and he instructed Sir William Bassett to destroy the images of St. Anne at Buxton and St. Andrew at Burton-on-Trent in Stafford-shire. With the assistance of his brother Francis, this he did, and in his own words '. . . that there should be no more idolatry and super-stition there used, I did not only deface the tabernacles and places where they did stand, but also did take away crutches, shirts and shifts, with wax offered, being things that allure and entice the ignorant . . .'. The images of the two saints were sent to Cromwell as proof that his instructions had been carried out. These images were probably more important than the waters, '. . . the fond trust thay did put in these images . . .', for from now on, the waters were enjoyed without the religious overtones.

The ill fated Mary, Queen of Scots visited the well on six occasions between 1573 and 1583 to seek relief from her chronic arthritis. At the time she was in the care of the Earl of Shrewsbury. Queen Elizabeth put an end to these visits for fear that Mary might be hatching a plot by meeting conspirators in this lonely place, a measure of Elizabeth's suspicion and fear. Mary it is said, scratched on a window the lines 'Buxtona, Quau calidae celbrabere nomine lymphae, Forte mihi post-ae non aduenda, vale'. of interest here is the expression 'calidae lymphae' meaning 'milk warm'; the temperature of the waters is 82°F (27.5°C), similar to freshly got milk.

Mary must have found her visits comforting. After her first visit she wrote 'I have not been at all disappointed, thank God', and later, when she heard of Elizabeth's suspicions, she protested '. . . before God that I have in this no object other than my health'.

The suspicion remained, probably because Buxton would have been an easy place from which to escape. Lord Burghley inspected the place in 1577 to check its security. The Earl of Shrewsbury gave an assurance in 1580 that the Queen's retinue were always under guard. Burghley tried the waters on his visit and commented, 'Mixt with sugar I find it potable with pleasure, even as whey'.

In 1572 a Dr. Jones published a treatise on the waters, from which it can be discerned that Buxton was very popular. In his 'Buckstone's Bathes Benefyte' he described a large bath house, with galleries and lodging for thirty persons. He recommends the appropriate pastimes, one being a wet weather game at the bath house. 'in the end of a bench eleven holes are made in the which to trowle pumments or bowles of leade, big, little, or mean or also of copper, tin, wood, either violent or soft, after their own discretion, the pastime of Trule in Madame is Termed'. A game that sounds similar to modern day bagatelle. It is comforting to learn that Dr. Jones, the eminent physician, declared that the waters, 'cureth most grievous diseases'.

The town itself must have been uninviting, for a traveller to Buxton in the 17th century referred to it as 'a waste and howling wilderness'. The bath house referred to by Dr. Jones was the Great Hall, built by the Earl of Shrewsbury. His descendant, William the 3rd Earl of Devonshire, replaced it with a larger hall. This was about the year 1670. The waters remained popular, but spas really came into their own at the turn of the 18th century. A charity was established in the reign of King George III known as the Buxton Bath Charity. This enabled the poor to seek relief from the waters. This later became the Devonshire Royal Hospital and Buxton Bath Charity, eventually to be absorbed into the National Health Service by the Act of 1948.

Those who could not afford the small fee payable, could seek and obtain free medical help. In 1844, for example, the poor were required to pay one shilling (5p) on each visit. The truly destitute could avail themselves of the waters with medicines, medical advice and an allowance of six shillings per week (30p) for three weeks. In the same year, over 1400 people were treated under the charity. It is reported that of these, some 1000 were cured or 'much relieved', 200 were 'relieved', 50 were 'no better' and the remainder 'remained on the books'.

In total some 10,000–12,000 persons visited Buxton each year to take the waters. To accommodate these numbers, the hotels and inns that abound in Buxton were built, and the baths were reconstructed on a larger scale in 1852.

The healing waters are the thermal waters, and these issue from the limestone at nine different places. It is said that these springs originate in the same subterranean source, where the water remains from 18 to 20 years. This water, apart from being radioactive is gaseous, mostly carbon dioxide and nitrogen, with a little argon and helium. These gases are more radioactive than the water, a characteristic known as radon. This is known elsewhere in Derbyshire and is a minor hazard in a fluorspar mine. The helium possibly originates from the clevite, which could also be the source of the radioactivity. An analysis made in 1912, by Sir Ernest Rutherford's principal assistant gave the following amounts of radium obtained from:

Gas 10.9 millionths of a milligram per litre.

Water 1.2 millionths of a milligram per litre.

The total output is approximately 3000 milli-microcuries per hour. There have been several analyses made of the waters, one of the latest by Beaumont Hart in 1920 showed:

	Grains per gallon	Grams per litre
Calcium carbonate	16.60	0.237
Magnesium bicarbonate	6.43	0.091
Ferrous bicarbonate	0.054	0.00077
Manganese bicarbonate	0.029	0.00041
Potassium sulphate	0.59	0.0084
Magnesium sulphate	0.78	0.0111
Sodium chloride	4.06	0.058
Ammonium chloride	0.006	0.000086
Magnesium chloride	0.42	0.006
Magnesium nitrate	0.09	0.003
Silica	0.60	0.0086
Oxygen gas	0.20	0.0029
Nitrogen gas	0.33	0.0047
Carbon acid gas	0.55	0.0078
Making a total of	30.739	0.439
Total dissolved salts	29.659	0.423

The present day visitor can see one of the springs, the one known as St. Anne's Well, where it flows into an oval marble basin in the Pump Room. This latter has been adapted into a Micrarium, but access to the spring is available independently. This building was built in 1894 to a neo-classical design by the architect, Henry Currey. Across the road is John Carr's crescent built exactly 100 years previously by the 5th Duke of Devonshire, reputedly from his share of the profits from his Ecton copper mines in Staffordshire.

The pump room was built as a place where people could take the waters in elegant surroundings and in congenial company. It is noticeable that the waters lack odour, they are tasteless, are free of organic matter and are of a strikingly blue colour. The visitor can sample them quite easily at the adjoining 'well of living waters', a monument to a councillor of the borough. It is not without good reason that the Buxton waters were rated second only to Bath in Somerset as a spa, and superior to all other spas, including Tunbridge Wells and Harrogate.

The waters at Buxton are the only true thermal waters in Derbyshire and one of only two in the country; the other is the one at Bath. Is it a coincidence that the Romans recognised this by naming these two places only, as Aquae, or did they know how to measure temperature? The definition of thermal waters, as suggested by the Institute of Geological Sciences, is those waters, which at the point of emergence have the same or a greater temperature than the mean average for the surrounding air. The pump room is at SK.058735, The Crescent, Buxton.

Matlock Bath

Some claim the thermal waters at Matlock Bath were to have been enjoyed by the Romans. Alas, there is little evidence of this, although the Romans were active in the area in pursuit of lead from the mines.

The earliest record of these springs is in 1698, although they were used by the Wolleys of Riber prior to this when a paved bath was built on to a spring by the Reverends Fern of Matlock and Henwood of Cromford. They passed this bath on to a George Wragg who paid a fine of £150 and an annual rent of six pence (2½p) on a 99 year lease from the Lords of the manor. Wragg enlarged the bath house making provision for visitors. The rooms he provided were apparently of poor quality and Wragg seems to have lost interest in the venture, for he sold the place to two Nottingham gentlemen by the name of Smith and Pennel, who paid nearly £1000 for it; a considerable profit for Wragg.

Messrs. Smith and Pennel built a lodging house and stables as well as a new bath house. They also converted the bridle road to Matlock Bridge into a carriage way and improved the road south to Cromford Bridge. Most of this now forms the trunk road, A6. Some time later a second spring was exploited, and to draw the distinction between the two, the former was named the Old Bath and the latter the New Bath. All the springs occur in a band 50 to 100 feet (15.2 to 30.48m) above the level of the River Derwent.

Plunge Pool, New Bath Hotel, Matlock Bath

Fountain in the
Pump Room
Matlock Bath

photo. H.M.Parker

The establishment of these baths and the number of visitors caused the owners to continue the carriageway south. A new road was blasted through Scarthin Rock, now called Scarthin Nick. A human skeleton with Roman coins was found in a cleft by workmen. The original bridle road south passed between the river and the rock to Cromford Bridge, passing through the now lost village of Willersley.

The Old Bath built by Smith and Pennel in 1734 was replaced in 1878 by a large gothic structure and called the Royal Hotel, later changed to the Royal Spa and Matlock Bath Hydro. This fine building burnt down in 1927, and the site is now occupied by the Temple Road car park. The famous grounds, once known as Dungeon Tors, Heights of Jacob and Romantic Rocks, are now part of Gulliver's Kingdom.

The spring that fed the Old Bath is now culverted, but the large volume of water still flows. It can be heard below a manhole cover in a grotto, once known as the Blue Grotto and with keystones engraved 'Royal Well founded 1696' on the car park (SK.293580), it appears on the surface as a picturesque waterfall on the side of the main road (SK.294581) where it descends into a pond, vanishes under the road, forms a second waterfall in the Pleasure Gardens, then feeds a further pond before overflowing into the river. At each waterfall it forms calcareous tufa, from which the grotto is built.

The New Bath Hotel occupies the site of a much earlier bath, which can still be seen in the basement. This hotel boasts a fine swimming pool fed from the same spring, which also supplies water to a fish pond in the grounds. The spring is above the hotel and is on private property. A further spring, also hidden, feeds the fishpond, which lies on the road side, near to the Grand Pavilion, SK.294582. The same spring once fed the Pump Room in the Pavilion, now an exhibition room. The 'pump', an elaborate porcelain tap housing, has been restored and can be seen to one side of the old pump room. but alas, water no longer issues from it. A fourth spring can be found in the garden of the Temple Hotel on Temple Road, SK.293582.

There are numerous other springs on this same hillside, and one more is worthy of mention as it is still in use. It originally fed the Fountain Baths, comprising a swimming pool, plunge and slipper baths. The iron skeleton of the pool can still be seen; the remainder of the building is now a gift shop and aquarium, where the various varieties of fish enjoy the spring water. The surplus water passes under the road and into the river where more fish can always be seen feeding off the waste matter.

The water that feeds the Fountain baths is not from a true spring but originates in a sough. The Fountain Bath Sough was driven in 1787 by a Dr. Simpson of Wentworth, West Yorkshire, who had bought the baths in 1780. This lead mine sough was driven into the Gilderoy

Mine on the Coal Pit Rake, and intersected the Wragg Sough which was discharging cold water. The latter was blocked with an iron gate, thus ensuring that the warm water flowed undiluted to the Fountain Bath. The Wragg Sough is named after the same George Wragg previously mentioned .

There is a further warm spring in the village on the east bank of the river; all the others are on the west bank. It lies behind the Grand Pavilion at SK.294582. This records a temperature of 17.4°C (63°F) some 2.4°C (5°F) cooler than its sisters across the valley.

There are three properties associated with the Matlock Bath waters. They are warm, usually 19.7 and 19.8°C (68°F) at the point of issue, somewhat cooler than the Buxton waters. (Any visitor to the village on a cold winter's day will see the steam rising from the fishpond and any other points where the water comes to the surface). They are radioactive, as the Buxton waters are; and they are 'petrifying'.

For a brief period, Matlock Bath enjoyed considerable popularity as a spa, with the added attractions of the magnificent tree lined gorge, the caverns and scenery. It was visited by Queen Victoria, and was popular with writers and artists, including Byron, Ruskin and Turner. It had a reputation for good health and longevity, both being ascribed to the consumption of the waters. One record states that 'Phthisis was unknown here' (pulmonary tuberculosis) and the death rate amongst the local inhabitants was given as 8.26 per thousand in the early 1920's.

Other Spas

The 'taking of the waters' became a popular diversion during the 19th century. Anyone could indulge and there were charities, similar to those at Buxton to help the poor. However, to enjoy the full treatment, one had to be fairly well off.

Such spas could make a lot of money for their owners, especially if they became fashionable. Tunbridge Wells, Cheltenham and Harrogate became very popular and the towns all grew as a consequence. Some people chose to live at these spas, and this accounts for some of the fine houses at Buxton and Matlock Bath. Spas in the continent were, and still are, very popular, as at the original Spa in Belgium, Baden-Baden, etc. Today, the visitors seem to place the waters at a lower level of importance to the other attractions of gambling, dining, and 'promenading'.

Others in Derbyshire had aspirations to compete with Buxton and Matlock Bath. They sprang up wherever warm water bubbled to the surface, and sometimes cold water. If it were warmer than normal, or had gases present, or were heavily mineralised, or all three, then it was considered fair game to be made into a spa.

Ilkeston Old Baths, illustration from Trueman's 'Ilkeston'

Some worthy of mention were:

Ashover chalybeate, with a reputation of flowing faster by night than by day!

Birley the owner, the Earl Manners erected seven baths here in 1843, situated in a wooded glen, 4½ miles (7 kilometres) south east of Sheffield city centre.This used to be part of Derbyshire but has now been ceded to the city. The area is commemorated by Birley Spa Lane, Hackenthorpe.

Bradwell a thermal spring behind Thatchers Inn and close to a caravan site was once enclosed in a bath house. This is now very ruinous and the water collects in a pool where it becomes brackish. Close by is the Roman settlement of Navio, near to Brough. The Romans no doubt knew of this spring and probably used it. (SK.174820).

Derby The Spa Inn on Abbey Street, stands near to a mineral spring discovered by a Doctor Chancey in 1733, whose cold waters bathed many a Derby townsperson.

Ilkeston a bath house was erected in 1830 on the present day Bath Street, to be enlarged in 1832 and 1845. The water was supposed to resemble Seltzer water as found at Selters in Germany, a form of soda water.

West Hallam little is known about this spa, where the waters were likened to those at Harrogate and Kedleston. Being within two miles of Ilkeston one can only conclude that the waters had the same origins in the coal measures.

Kedleston adjoining Quarndon is Kedleston Park and Hall, seat of the Curzons. A cool sulphur spring, 8.3°C (47°F), was discovered in the park and was duly enclosed in a fine structure. Lord Denman compared this water with that at Tunbridge Wells and he considered the Kedleston water to be 'efficatious in scorbutic and cutaneous diseases', (scurvy and skin conditions). The water was valued as a remedy for gout and was sold in the streets of Derby for that purpose. The townspeople must have thought highly of it, for it was used 'as a substitute for malt liquor!'. A remarkable water indeed! The charge for carriage was a penny a quart. Kedleston Hotel was built in anticipation of a good trade in visitors. This was not fulfilled and the hotel was for many years a farm house before becoming a hotel again. A Doctor T. Short, writing in 1734, said that the waters 'stank horribly', this would have been a 'bad eggs' smell.

Quarndon a chalybeate spring in this village lies on the road to Derby (SK.333407) and is protected by a three arched gothic structure. Sometimes a little water issues from a lion's mouth. A plate records a famous visitor, '17th Century Chalybeate Spring Well, Once Famous Spa noted for Medicinal Waters Containing Iron. Visited by Daniel Defoe in 1727'. The waters ceased to flow after an earthquake in 1896. Chalybeate is a common expression for iron bearing water.

Shuttlewood these springs were very sulphurous and were similar to Harrogate waters. They were situated near to a farmhouse known as the Nunnery, 2 miles (3 kilometres) north by north west of Bolsover, to the side of the Stanfree to Clowne road. There is evidence of a spring in a wood here, but the bath house has gone (SK. 471734).

Stoney Middleton It is said that the Romans knew of the spring waters here. Under the gardens of a housing development lie the foundations of a Roman villa, and the overflow from the well runs through these gardens, so there might be some truth in it. The spring is thermal at 64°F (17.7°C) and is to be seen close to the church at SK.232756. There used to be three springs and Doctor Short reported in 1734, 'three perpetually bubbling warm springs, close to the west side of the church'. At one time, it was reputed to have curative properties, particularly for rheumatism.

The Chalybeate Well, Quarndon

A crusader, who returned from the Middle East with leprosy, was supposedly cured by these waters. In all probability, if the tale be true, he had a skin disorder which washing in any water would have cured. He was grateful enough to cause a chapel to be built, dedicated to Saint Martin, the crusader's patron saint, out of gratitude for being relieved of such a fearful disease. The present church of Saint Martin occupies the site of the chapel, and has an unusual octagonal plan. The well is dressed each year, and an unusual feature is the spreading of flowers on the floor of the church in the form of a crucifix.

Wirksworth to the west of the road to Derby was once a sulphur spring, which Doctor Short described, 'Wirksworth black sulphur-water is famous not only for Cutaneous disorders, but also for Rheums of the eyes and Scrophulous Disorders . . . its water is very black.' This later claim appears to be against the monarch's perquisite of touching for the King's Evil (scrofula).

Allen Hill 'Spaw Restored', Matlock

Spaw Restored

A strongly chalybeate 'spring' at the bottom of the Dimple at Matlock, (SK.296604) is a mine sough driven into shale. It sits in a small garden with trees and shrubs. One assumes that it must have healing properties for inscribed over its stone portal are the words, '1824 Allen Hill Spaw Restored'. One can only speculate at the reason for this! Allen Hill is the name of the hill from which the water issues — or is it the name of grateful man who rediscovered his potency?

The water is channelled away, and the degree of the iron present can be seen by the heavy deposit of sinter on the channel and on articles, usually rubbish, left in the water.

Hydros

Mr. John Smedley (1803 – 74) of Lea Mills, Lea Bridge, was a hosiery manufacturer whose health broke down in 1851. The treatment by physicians having had little or no effect on his malady, believed to

49

have been a nervous breakdown, he sought a cold water cure at Harrogate in Yorkshire. He was apparently cured of his illness, and he returned to his mill at Lea Bridge, so full of enthusiasm that he evolved a method of treatment which he practiced on his long suffering work people.

Matlock Bank which overlooks Matlock from the east, is built partly on an outcrop of shale, capped by millstone grit with a limestone underlayer. Nearly the whole of the east side of the Derwent Valley is so formed. Surface water percolates through the grit, which outcrops in numerous places forming the well known 'edges'. The shale is impervious to water, thus springs occur at regular intervals along the top edge of this shale. There are two adjoining fields in Matlock Bank. The upper one is known as Wellfield and lies on top of the shale. Those requiring water had to sink wells into the water table, which formed above the shale. The lower field was known as Springfield, where the water came to the surface off the shale. Wellfield is now occupied by allotment gardens, Springfield by a new development of houses on an access road named Springfield Rise.

Smedley had noted these springs, particularly those at Matlock Bank, where in 1853 he purchased a cottage where he installed baths and commenced his hydropathic treatment. This, it is claimed, founded modern hydropathy and put Matlock on the map. The cottage was bought as a going concern, as it was already being operated as a hydro by a Ralph Davis of Darley Dale, who commenced his treatment two years prior to Smedley. This cottage boasted eleven rooms and housed six patients. Smedley gradually outgrew this cottage, which he extended and finally rebuilt. In 1859, the establishment had 76 bedrooms, and by 1863 over 1000 patients were being treated each year. A second extension, built in 1867 added a further 94 bedrooms. It is a memorial to the man that he designed and built all the buildings himself.

One of the springs that fed this establishment still supplies a beautiful grotto in what was the Summer House, now occupied by the Architect's Department of the Derbyshire County Council.

Smedley added flair and imagination to his hydro, out of which his unrivalled success was created. His methods were crude and spartan by modern standards. Religious observance was a prerequisite for the patient, food was simple and the treatment could be uncomfortable in the extreme. In spite, or because of, this, the name Smedley became famous, and a by-word for integrity.

When Doctor W. B. Hunter took charge in 1872, many of Smedleys rules were relaxed. The social side of hydropathy was improved and the tennis and bowls courts were laid out. Smedley would have been

A drainage well near Brassington, sunk by
traditional methods some thirty years ago

appalled at the Christmas dances, and the availability of alcohol and
tobacco. Hunter died in 1894, but the cure continued, with an
interruption during World War II, until the National Health Act. This
Act of 1948 did not recognise hydropathy, and this coupled with a
change in fashion in such methods, and the high cost of the treatment, caused Smedleys to be closed. People with money preferred to
channel their energies into more fashionable pursuits. Where Smedley
led, there were those who were certain to follow his example, for
without doubt, he made a lot of money out of his hydro.

A Charles Rowland opened Rockside Hydro in 1862, which contains work by an architect R. Barry Parker who later designed the first
garden city at Letchworth. Rockside is now part of the Matlock
College of Education, as is the Chatsworth Hydro. Lillybank Hydro is
now part of the Presentation Convent School. There were lesser
establishments; Chesterfield House Hydro, Oldham House and Pros-
pect Place. Even the Old Bath Hotel at Matlock Bath tried to cash in on
the boom by renaming it the Royal Spa and Matlock Bath Hydro.

In the 1920's the charges varied from £4 4s (£4.20) to £6 6s (£6.30) per
week for full board, treatment being extra. Smedley's was one of the
cheapest.

The nearby villages were quick to copy too; Ashover House Hydro at Ashover, Grand Hotel and Hydro at Baslow, Clarke's at Darley Dale, now St. Elphin's School.

The effect of these establishments on Matlock Bank was considerable. The community grew from a few cottages just prior to Smedley to a large town by the turn of the century. The hydros employed large numbers of people. A tramway was built up Bank Road, which carried passengers up for two pence and down for a penny. This was operated by cable, the drum for which was driven by a steam engine housed at the top of Bank Road. The house for this is extant just below Rockside Hydro, and is now used as a garage. The lower terminus was at Crown Square, the shelter is preserved in the adjoining Hall Leys Park. It was fashioned on the Cable Cars at San Francisco, the idea of George Newnes the publisher, born at Matlock Bath. What an attraction this would have been were it still operational today.

Smedley's Hydro is now the offices of the Derbyshire County Council, and dominates the town of Matlock. It is substantially as it stood as a hydro, the renowned bowling and tennis courts are now alas, car parking areas.

Derbyshire Neck

In spite of so many claims that the waters in Derbyshire had such curative properties, the water in some districts could cause a disease. 'Derbyshire Neck' was once a common sight, causing severe disfigurement. This was a local name for a goitre, a swelling of the thyroid gland, due, it is believed to a shortage of iodine in spring water. It was endemic in the limestone uplands of the county, and has been eradicated by an improvement in diet and piped water.

CHAPTER FIVE

Soughs

Introduction

Wherever man has delved into the earth to exploit the mineral rich strata, he has encountered many problems, the chief of which was water. As miners sank mines deeper into the ground they penetrated the various water tables and as a consequence the workings became very wet and were frequently drowned. The miner was an unwilling well sinker, digging beyond the water table. So bad could this become that summer working only would be possible in some mines, whilst in others the working had to be abandoned, often with the forfeiture of rich deposits.

Early attempts at pumping consisted of bailing, a slow and laborious method, or by rag and chain pump. Both needed constant attention from teams of workmen and consequently they cost large sums of money. A better solution was the sough, a near horizontal tunnel or adit, driven from the lowest possible level in a nearby valley, and driven to intersect the mine workings at depth, as far below the water table as possible. Initially soughs were very costly, but often repaid their cost with dividends. The water would then drain from the workings, flowing out of the sough and free unworked deposits for exploitation. They were, therefore, instrumental in lowering the water tables in the hills of the Pennines, with the consequences that we have inherited. The reduction of tree density in the uplands, and the drying up of some springs are but two of the unwanted products of sough driving.

Soughs are therefore, man-made springs, and Derbyshire is justifiably famous for them. The subject of soughs, their finance, surveying, digging and operation is the subject for a book in itself. Here, we must content ourselves with those soughs which were important, or which have found different uses than just mine draining.

The idea of using soughs as drainage tunnels is an ancient one and in many respects Derbyshire led the world in this technology. The Russet Well at Castleton, is technically a sough in that it drains mines, but it is not man made. Some soughs tapped thermal waters, and the water that issues from these is still thermal, e.g. Stoke Sough — 11.6°C, Meerbrook Sough — 15.3°C, Ridgeway Sough — 14.1°C, and Fountain Bath Sough — 19.7°C (see chapter 4). A Sough may be many miles in length and some had one or more branches. The grid references given are for the portals of the soughs, the point where the waters issues, or as the old miners would say 'comes to day'.

Meerbrook Sough (SK.327552)

This sough, without its branches is 2½ miles long, 5 miles with its branches but is not the longest in Derbyshire. Hillcarr Sough is 3 miles long, 9 with its branches. It drains the lead veins and mines in the Wirksworth Basin and the surrounding hills. Its line marked by a row of draw shafts now covered with stone 'beehives'. Water vapour still rises from these in frosty weather. This sough is now a water supply, being inaugurated on 24th July, 1904 as the Ilkeston and Heanor Water Board, the cermony being performed by the then mayor of Ilkeston Mr. F. Sudbury.

Prior to this venture Ilkeston drew its water partly from Stanley Brook and partly from Peacock Colliery. These supplies proved inadequate for the needs of the growing town. Likewise Heanor had taken its water supplies from the Bailey Brook Colliery shaft, supplemented by bores at Smalley Hill. Prior to these sources being tapped the town had used a colliery shaft at Langley Mill, and earlier still a well at Waterloo Rock, Commonside.

A roadside attraction

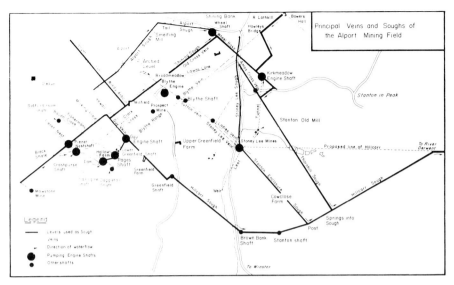

Courtesy of the Peak District Mines Historical Society Ltd.

Cromford

The earliest lead mine soughs of any importance were driven in Cromford early in the 17th century. The mines above Cromford on the hill overlooking the village from the west, had been worked down to the water table, particularly on the Gang and Godbehere Veins, which run parallel with, and to the north of, the old Cromford and High Peak Railway, now the High Peak Trail.

To continue working these veins meant having to lower the water table in the hill below the Black Rocks, known at the time as the Stonnis. The picnic area below Black Rocks is the site of the Cromford Moor Mine, the capped shaft of which is still evident, near to the public toilets. To undertake their first sough the miners called in a Dutchman, one Sir Cornelius Vermuyden, who had been knighted for his work in draining Hatfield Chase in the Isle of Axholme. Land drainage was a 'cause celebre' during the early part of the 17th century. He it was, who drove the first major sough in Derbyshire, for draining the Dove Gang Vein. It took ten years to drive, from 1631 to 1641, and it was driven through mineral veins. The portal is now lost.

The next sough was Bates Sough, sometimes referred to as Longhead or Cromford Moor Old Sough, driven 1653 to 1654. It took so little time because it was possibly dug through shale, a soft and easy material to mine. The portal of this is also lost, although there is strong evidence of it as a spring in a private garden on Bede House Lane.

55

The next sough to be driven, through shale, was the Cromford Sough, started about 1672. This connected to the Gang Vein with branches to the Vermuyden and Bates Soughs, which were now at a higher altitude. This is probably why the portals are lost, as they would have reduced in volume considerably.

The portal of Cromford Sough can be seen at SK.296569 from whence a good flow of clear water issues. It is contained within a walled enclosure, to the rear of the tea room facing Cromford Market Place. The water from the pool on Water Lane, (overlooked by Scarthin Books) is culverted after passing over a weir and mixes with the sough water which is also culverted. The stream was once on the surface and was forded, hence the name of the village. It was Arkwright who sent the water underground, in 1790.

The mixed waters are conveyed through the village and pass over Mill Lane in an iron aqueduct to supply the wheels in the mill. Both are in situ and the wheels are now undergoing restoration. Arkwright chose this site for his mill having had a troublesome time in Nottingham due to frame breakers. He believed that he would experience less trouble at Cromford, but he was cautious enough to make the ground floor of his new mill windowless. This mill replaced an earlier paper mill which also used the mixed water.

Cromford Sough Tail

Arkwright was also attracted to this water because it had the reputation of never running dry in summer or freezing in winter. This was due to the sough waters being of high volume at the time and slightly thermal. The surplus water discharged into the Coal Wharf of the Cromford Canal nearby, as a feeder. These water channels with their feeders and sluices can still be seen adjacent to Mill Lane. It was said that 'due to the temperature of the sough water the canal remained navigable during severe frost'.

The water volume from Cromford Sough diminished considerably after the Meerbrook Sough opened, for the Gang vein branch of this sough connected with this vein, the water table being lowered yet further by 100ft (30m). Arkwright entered into a long drawn out legal battle to have the water restored, to no avail.

At the far end of North Street, adjacent to the school, is a sough-like portal now blocked up, with a pipe from which a small trickle of water discharges into a stone trough. This was the water supply to the Arkwright houses on North Street and may be connected to one of the soughs.

The water wheel on Water Lane at the head of the pool was used to drive a baryte mill, and this was driven by water from Alabaster Sough. This latter ranges through the hillside opposite towards the village of Middleton-by-Wirksworth and drains a mine of the same name.

Cromford Village once derived its water supplies from several small springs, one of these was the Roguelen Spring, a supply from the Roggelim Mine, (SK.294562). A spring near to this supplied the upper levels of Matlock Bath.

Lathkill Dale

This beautiful dale was once the scene of frantic mining activity, particularly the Mandale Mine, the adit entrance to which is west of Over Haddon at SK.198662. The inexperienced are warned not to enter these workings, they look harmless but are very unstable and dangerous.

Close to the mine can be seen a water wheel pit which housed a 35 feet (10.7m) diameter overshot wheel which drove a pump, erected in 1840. There is also the ruins of an engine house, built in 1847, which housed a 160hp, (119kW) Cornish pumping engine, removed in 1852. Both in their turn pumped water out of the lower workings and into the sough. The water which drove the wheel came from a spring in Cales Dale. The leet that carried this water can still be traced; the stone piers crossing the river once carried a wooden launder or aqueduct for conveying the spring water across the valley.

The sough was started in 1797 or 1798 and progress was slow. The miners or soughers frequently encountered bad ground which reduced progress to four or five yards (3.7-4.6m) a week, using a gang of eight men. A driving rate at Ecton Copper Mines at the same time, with the same number of men, was eight to ten yards (7.3-9.1m) per week. By 1820 the work was completed, probably at a loss, for the cost was as high if not higher than the returns.

Water still flows out of the mile long Mandale Sough in wet weather during autumn, winter and spring, but it is dry, as is the River Lathkill, during summer. The water from the sough is conveyed in a leet to join the river downstream, a precaution against poisoning the fish, for this is a famous trout river. The grille is to prevent the trout swimming into the sough.

Another sough in the same dale, the Lathkill Dale Sough, was driven along a lead vein or rake of the same name which runs east/west along the valley. The portal collapsed many years ago but its position can be found downstream of Lathkill Lodge at SK.205661, where a spring appears amidst disturbed ground, close to the re-emergence of the river at the Bubbling Spring. The depressions to the north edge of the path upstream of Mandale Mine are collapsed shafts on the Lathkill Dale Sough. A recently installed manhole gives access into the sough, and the bird bath in the garden of the Lathkill Lodge is sited on a shaft lying on the sough. The ruins at SK.194658, south of the river and east of Mandale Mine are the remains of a mine agent's house named Bateman's House in his memory. This house lies immediately above the sough, and is connected by two shafts, one of which once housed a unique 'disc' engine, a form of simple turbine patented by the Dakeyne Brothers in 1830. These inventors were flax millers at Darley Dale.

An editor of the Mechanics Magazine in 1833 commented on the specification for this engine, 'a perfect smother of outlandish jargon'. Such a machine would have been difficult to operate, it being estimated that its design head of 66 feet of water (20m) would give a working pressure of 25.5lb per square inch (1.76 bar). The water for driving this engine probably came from the same leet that supplied Mandale Mine.

Much higher up the dale where it gives way to Fern Dale, can be seen an attempt at a sough that failed. By the side of the footpath along the dale towards Monyash are the blocks of stone left by the men who worked Ricklow Quarry for 'Derbyshire Figured Marble', a crinoidal limestone and not a true marble. To the north of the path at SK.165661 can be seen an opening in a cliff face inscribed 'I.B.1787'. The initials are those of Isaac Berresford and the sough is named after him. Alternative names are Barsett's Cut or Ricklow Mine. This attempt to unwater Magpie Mine near Sheldon (SK.172682) was abandoned.

Household Pump, Brassington

Wood-cased Pump at the Miners Arms
Brassington

Magpie Sough

An attempt to drain the mine of the same name has been mentioned above. A more serious attempt was started on the south bank of the River Wye, one mile (1.km) west of Ashford-in-the-Water in 1873. It was the last major sough in Derbyshire and is notable for the pioneering of the use of pneumatic drills and nitroglycerine in the county. The enterprise took eight years to complete and was a financial disaster. The cost of this sough has been estimated as being as low as £8,000 and as high as £35,000. The actual cost was probably about £18,000, a considerable sum in those days, during a period when lead was falling in price. The going was hard for the soughers for they were driving through toad-stone, a volcanic lava, for much of the way. This is a hard stone and is very difficult to mine.

In 1874, Richard Schram erected a water wheel in the river to drive the compressor for working his pneumatic drills. He used his own men, who could not cope with the conditions. After four disappointing months, Schram sold his machinery to the mining company for £250. The soughers managed better than Schram's men for they used the machinery throughout the driving of the sough. The sough-ers encountered powerful springs and when they broke into the workings on 18th August, 1881, a head of 108 feet (33m) of water was released through a pilot hole. So great was the force of this water, 47 lb. per square inch (3.22 bar) that it extinguished the sougher's lights and they had to flee for their lives, 'the water followed them at considerable speed'.

At the turn of the century a boat 24 feet (7.3m) long and 4 feet (1.22m) in the beam was used in the sough for conveying up to 2½ tons (2540 kg.) of ore out of the mine. The boat exited with the flow of the water assisting; the return trip of the empty boat was made by 'legging' the vessel, canal style.

Lock gates were erected in the sough to maintain sufficient water for this purpose. The owner organised Sunday excursions in this boat at two shillings and six pence (12½p) per head, probably being as profit-able at this price as mining the lead. It was more than a day's wages for some.

This sough is open for its whole length of 1¼ miles (2 km), access is prohibited and the sough is very dangerous. The entance collapsed in 1966 and was dug out in 1974 by the Peak District Mines Historical Society Ltd. The present portal is therefore modern. A large volume of clear water still issues out of the sough, measured as 7½ million gallons per day (34 million litres per day) in 1967, and as 8-9½ m.g.d. (38.6-43.1 m.l.d.) in 1929. It must be draining a considerable catch-ment west of Bakewell. For comparison, Meerbrook Sough discharges approximately twice as much.

Hillcarr Sough

This sough borrows its technology from the Worsley Coal Mines, for two of the shareholders were John Barker, a renowned lead smelter who had visited the Worsley Mines and the Bridgewater Canal; and a John Gilbert, agent to the Duke of Bridgewater, who had managed the construction of the underground canal system at Worsley. Another shareholder was Peter Nightingale of Lea, another smelter and a relative of the famous Florence.

Hillcarr Sough is 4½ miles (7.24km) long and was driven through shale for ease of working. The sough is unusually large, up to ten feet (3m) high in places, and the soughers used boats for haulage with fans for ventilation, ideas borrowed from the Coal mines at Worsley.

Work commenced in June 1766 and by 1769 it had penetrated 3000 feet (915m) from its portal, a different driving rate than Magpie Sough! It then turned south west for ¾ mile (1206m) to avoid the limestone and to join Stanton and Brown Bank Shafts. From the latter it was driven north west to intersect Greenfield Shaft in 1783. This rubbish-filled shaft is near Lower Greenfield Farm at SK.220638. This sough was navigable to this shaft by using punt-like boats. By the time it had reached Guy Vein in 1787, (SK.219637), it had taken 21 years of work at a cost of £32,000.

The standard of the surveying must have been exceptional for the soughers to intersect mine shafts at such distances, particularly as ventilation shafts were not used.

Branches were driven to unwater other mines, Thornhill Sough, Stanton Enclosure Sough and an extension to Mawstone Mine, near Bradford, the scene of an explosion in 1932 when seven men died. A scheme was put forward in 1922 to extend this sough to the Lathkill Dale and Magpie Mines, but was not instituted. During the driving of the sough, underground springs near to the Thornhill Sough were tapped causing Plackett Mine at Winster to be unwatered, two miles (3.2 km) distant to the south.

John Taylor, the great mining engineer, suggested that Hillscarr Sough discharged the greatest quantity of water of any sough in the history of mining; an obvious over-statement, but it does discharge large quantities of water. In 1929 the discharge was calculated as 7-8 m.g.d. (32-36 m.l.d.), a little less than Magpie Sough. In 1967, a flow rate of 4.25 m.g.d. (19.3 m.l.d.) was recorded. The portal is on the west bank of the River Derwent at SK.259637, a mile up-stream of Darley Bridge.

Speedwell Level

In this disused lead mine, now a show cave, the visitor can experience a boat journey on an underground canal, modelled on the Worsley Coal Mines. This level was driven south towards Longcliff between 1774 and 1781. The water that feeds this canal is from several stream caves near New Rake. The entrance is at the foot of the Winnats Pass, Castleton at SK.139827.

Russet Well, Castleton

Whilst in Castleton a visit to Peak Cavern is essential. It was one of the 'Wonders of the Peak', once indelicately known as the 'Devil's Arse o' Peak. This huge natural cavern houses a famous rope walk, and from its mouth issues a strong stream, known as Peakshole Water. On the east side of the access path is the Russet Well, a spring which drains to the lead veins and mines to the west of the gorge. The water must therefore pass below the Peakshole Water and gorge before rising. This then acts as a natural sough.

An Underground Well

Lead miners frequently formed wells in the mine workings, by penetrating a water table with a shallow shaft. These are common-place, but inaccessible to most people. One such can be seen with ease, within the Great Rutland Cavern at Matlock Bath, first opened to the public as a show cave in 1810. This well appears to have been devised as a well and not a flooded mine shaft. The water was used for washing ore underground, in the days when the cavern was known as the Nestus Mine, 'the apparatus is supplied with streams of water from the first fish ponds, where gold, and silver, and River Fish, are living in perpetual darkness'. This was written in 1818. The cavern has enjoyed an uninterrupted popularity from when it first opened, and has been visited by large parties of people from time to time. Three hundred Sunday School children paid a visit in 1858 and made tea from this well in a 30 gallon (136 litres) tea pot which they had brought with them.

Visitors still make a wish at the well, now called Jacob's Well, but the tradition of casting money into the well is dying out. The water is clean and very cold and never changes in character. The level of the water remains constant regardlesss of the weather, even throughout the drought of 1976.

Great Rutland Cavern is to be found at Matlock Bath, high on the hillside known as the Heights of Abraham, (laid out when the 'picturesque' movement was popular in Victorian times and so named due to its supposed similarity with the hill of the same name, stormed by Wolfe of Quebec).

Within the cavern is an area called Roger Rain's House where water rains in through the roof. This water soaks through from a spring in Cave Dale above. It is thought by some that this spring could have been used as a water supply for Perveril Castle nearby. This ruin, built by William Peveril and immortalised by Sir Walter Scott, was apparently without a well or spring within the fortifications. As it was built to withstand a siege a water supply would have been essential. The Russet Well is at SK.148828; the spring in Cave Dale at SK.150826.

CHAPTER SIX

A Miscellany of Wells and Springs

Petrifying Wells

The thermal waters of Matlock Bath have for centuries deposited tufa on the hillside to a great depth. The New Bath Hotel and the Grand Pavilion are both built on it. It outcrops on the roadside and has been used extensively in the locality for walling stone. The highly mineralised water 'petrifies' anything in its path. The tufa is petrified vegetation with additional deposits of lime. It forms encrustations, which can become large where the water is presented with a large air surface.

Good examples of this can be seen as banks of tufa at waterfalls, where the spring water discharges into the River Derwent, behind the Grand Pavilion car park, and into ponds as at the side of Temple Road, the Pleasure Gardens opposite, and the fountain in the Fish Pond.

Tufa supports vegetable life with the addition only of water, and the rich green moss-covered tufa is very distinctive. This made it popular with the Victorians, who used tufa as rockery stone, especially in grottos. The grotto in the Temple Road car park is made from tufa as is the grotto in the Architect's Department in the County Offices at Matlock, both mentioned elsewhere. A small but busy industry was created in the 19th century in quarrying and transporting tufa. It is still sold at garden centres, cut and set with plants.

This ability for the water to coat objects with lime, as at the bottom of a domestic kettle, was exploited, and several petrifying wells were established at Matlock Bath. Into these wells were placed everyday objects; umbrellas, eggs in nests, teapots, boots, bird cages, etc. After a year or so these would be completely coated in lime, giving the impression that the object had been turned to stone. These were removed and sold to the public in nearby shops.

Only one of these wells remains, and unfortunately its future may be doubtful. The present very modern structure, which replaced an earlier one, and the adjoining fountain are at the north end of the Riverside Gardens, fronting the A6 road to Matlock (SK.294582). There are other petrifying springs in the area. The Dunsley Springs of which there are two, are high above the Via Gellia, near to the hamlet of Slaley. One originates in a lead mine, the Dunsley Level, now closed off with a steel door for it is also a water supply (SK.268568). A bank of tufa descends to the roadside, supporting a luxuriant growth

At the source of the Bradwell Brook

'Tidi's Well', Tideswell

Little John's Well, Longshaw Estate
Nether Padley

High Well, Taddington
vandalised in Spring 1982

of grasses and mosses. The spring water cascades down the bank and under the road, the A5012. On this bank is a cottage, built of tufa but erroneously named Marl Cottage. For many years it was a game-keeper's cottage, for this valley was once part of the Gell estate. The tufa was quarried extensively above Marl Cottage and there is still a little evidence of this remaining.

It is sad to reflect that there is only one surviving petrifying well in the county, and this might be threatend. This phenomenon is exploited to the full in Savonnerieres in France, where plaques are made in the 16th century petrifying grottos. They use resin moulds made from old bronze tableaux, coated with wax and placed in lime-laden water for up to three years. The end result, when the mould is removed, is a one inch thick copy of the original which has an ivory like patina. These are imported and sold at Matlock — how much more pleasant it would be if they were produced locally.

Ebbing and Flowing Wells

As the name implies, these springs have the rare distinction that the water rises and falls spontaneously, or is supposed to. There are two of these wells in Derbyshire, one at Tideswell, the other at Barmoor Clough. The one at Tideswell is the third of the Seven Wonders of the Peak. It lies in a rockery in a private garden on the Manchester Road. Some have expressed a preference for the well at Barmoor Clough to be the wonder, for it is reputed to have worked. The one at Tideswell is a very dubious affair. Charles Cotton must have found its per-formance lacking for he wrote of it, 'This fountain is so small, the observer hardly can perceive it crawl!'

The one at Barmoor is more easily seen, for it lies to the side of the Dove Holes to Sparrowpit road, the A623 (SK.085797). It is situated below the road on its south side, opposite to an entrance to Bennetston Hall Hotel. The well is walled to the hillside, and a series of troughs can still be seen, forming the arc of a circle.

J. B. Frith wrote in 1905, 'The pool is but a few inches deep, for the most part covered with scum, and, as the cattle come here to drink, the adjoining ground is often a muddy quagmire and the well altogether is most uninspiring'. It has changed not at all in nearly eighty years. It is probably choked now from neglect, as eye witnesses used to vouchsafe for it working. The frequency of its operation varied greatly from every few minutes to several days, this being no doubt dependant on the amount of water in the ground, for after an extremely dry spell, it would take several weeks to operate.

One record gives some detail of the well's performance. The flow would start slowly and accelerate, the flow lasting for four and a half minutes. It was said that it discharged 20 hogsheads of water in a minute, (1260 gallons per minute, 95.5 litres per second) some of it ebbing back to its source, the remainder running under the road to a pond. It was considered a miraculous happening for years, some even believed that the wells were linked with the sea. It is a syphoning action, no different to that employed in the design of the Tantalus Cup, a novelty once imported from China. This comprised a cup, which contained the figure of a man, illustrating the principle of the syphon. It derives its name from Tantalus, son of Zeus who was condemned to stand in water which reached his chin. When he bent his head for a drink, the water receded, whence 'tantalising'.

It was commonly believed that Tideswell was named after its ebbing and flowing i.e. tidal well. This alas was not so. The village is named after an ancient local of the name Tidi. Nearby can be found Tideslow, Tidi's burial place or ground. A well at Tideswell was once known as the Weeding Well, where withies grew. This, it is assumed is the one that gave the village its name. It is now culverted under Fountain Square. One could only wish that they might be dug out and made to work again.

Sources of the Rivers Dove and Derwent

In the vicinity of Axe Edge, four rivers are born, the Dane, Goyt, Manifold and Dove. Of these only the Dove rises in Derbyshire and spends its whole life in the county. It forms the boundary between Derbyshire and Staffordshire, so half of its width lies inside and half outside the county.

All rivers start in a humble way, and none more so than the Dove. It commences its life at Dove Head Farm on the Buxton to Leek road, the A53 at SK.032685. Pass through the gate opposite the farm, over the stile to the left and the Dove Head Spring is to found inside a stone built portal. An inscription on the lintel bears the initials of Charles Cotton and Isaac Walton, whose fishing exploits on the Dove are legendary. These marks date from the middle of the 19th century.

It was Cotton who wrote of the Dove;

> 'O my beloved Nymph, fair Dove!
> Princess of rivers! How I love
> Upon thy flowery banks to lie!'

Much has been said of Dove Dale, and Byron summed it all up in a note to Tom Moore, 'Was you ever in Dovedale? I assure you there are

Dunsley Spring, Via Gellia, near Slaley — Troughs at Ible

Well above the Via Gellia used by D.H.Lawrence
during his stay at Mountain Cottage

things in Derbyshire as noble as in Greece or Switzerland'. An exaggeration perhaps, but lovers of Dovedale would not disagree. It inspired Walton's 'The Compleat Angler', Cotton, Moore and others. The literature about the Dove is considerable and there is no place for it here. Suffice it that a quotation from Drayton's 'Polyolbion' completes the subject admirably;

'To the Staffordian fields doth rove,
visits the springs of Trent and Dove'.

The river Derwent rises in the Dark Peak and its entire life is spent in Derbyshire, joining the Trent east of Great Wilne, close to Shardlow. Its course takes it through Chatsworth Park, the Matlocks and Derby, collecting the waters of the Wye on its way.

Its actual source is hard to determine, for upwards of ten springs on Ronksley Moor could lay claim to the honour. These springs are all close to each other and are known collectively as Swains Greave. The likeliest candidate is a spring at SK.127975.

The moors in this area abound in springs and they run either into the Derwent valley or the Etherow from springs on Featherbed Moss. The Don also rises in this area but outside the county.

There are other springs outside the county but close by, which feed the Derwent before it spills into Howden Reservoir, and they carry such names as Hoar Clough Spring, Horse Shoe Spring, Bull Stones Spring, Lord Surrey's Spring and Lord Edward Howard's Spring. These were probably so named after being visited or used by grouse shooting parties; the Howard family, the Dukes of Norfolk, are big land owners in the area. One of the Dukes was responsible for Glossop's first water supply from springs above Swineshaw Reservoir (SK.043958) overlooking Old Glossop.

An Emergence and Resurgence

The Lathkill a picturesque but short river, comes to the surface at Lathkill Head Cave east of Monyash at SK.171659. This cave, which has an explored length of 2000 feet, (610m) must not be explored except in the company of experts. It is also known as Lathkill House Cave and Ricklow Cavern, the latter incorrectly. Water issues from this cave from early autumn to late spring, at other times it is dry, as is the river. This strange phenomenon also occurs with the river Manifold over the border in Staffordshire. The water re-appears further down stream at the Bubbling Spring, upstream of Conksbury Bridge. (SK.205661). Meanwhile the river pursues an underground course. The water originates in nearby Knotlow Lead Mine.

Close to Where a Cavalier Fell

The Bradford, shorter than the Lathkill into which it runs, passes through a series of man-made fish pools, the haunt of the dipper and wagtail, with many a fine trout to be seen. It rises as a spring at the foot of a rock cave near to Middleton-by-Youlgreave and was once the water supply for Middleton, the pipe for which is still in situ.

Close by this spot a tragedy of the Civil War occurred. A local Royalist, Christopher Fulwood, espoused the cause of Charles I, and raised an army of 1100 local men. Hearing of this the Governer of the County, Sir John Gell of Hopton, sought to capture him. A group of Roundheads chased Fulwood from his home at Middleton, cornering him in a cave close to the spring, known as Fulwood's or Cromwell's Cave. He was shot and wounded. He died as a captive on the 6th November 1643 whilst enroute to Lichfield.

Mompesson's Well

The Eyam plague is one of Derbyshire's best known events and has been the subject of numerous books, articles, television and radio programmes. The tragedy is well known to most people and is adequately and ably covered elsewhere.

Next to Saint Anne's Well at Buxton, Mompesson's Well is the best known one in the county. Here it was that the beleaguered villagers left money in return for food brought in from adjoining parishes. They endured voluntary isolation whilst the Great Plague ravaged the village from September 1665 to October 1666. The village suffered grievously during this period, but its Rector the Reverend William Mompesson persuaded the people to persevere, and he was their comfort and inspiration. He had the foresight to evacuate his own two children before the disease got a hold. His wife Catherine stayed with him and perished.

The food supplies left at the well were organised by the then Lord Lieutenant of the County, the Duke of Devonshire. The villagers left money in payment in vinegar as a mild disinfectant. Soon after the plague had spent itself, Mompesson took up the living of Eakring in Nottinghamshire, becoming a Prebend of York and Southwell. He died in 1708.

The well is a rectangular shallow trough which contains a sturdy spring. It is protected by an iron fence and is remote from the village, on the hill top close to Ladywash Mine. Had it not been so far from Eyam, it would not have been used as a depository for food for the adjoining terrified villagers, SK.223774.

The memorial well to James Brindley, Canal Engineer, at Wormhill

Etwall

A spring with a well lies by the church, close to the caretaker's house for the John Port School. The spring is enclosed in a large and monumental stone sarcophagus, measuring fifteen feet (5.57m) by five feet (1.52m), with a solid hip roof. It is a considerable structure for housing a spring. Through one open end, where there was once a door, can be seen the water and a pipe complete with a strainer basket and foot valve, evidence that the water has been pumped. The spring overflows into a well or dipping trough, a very unhygienic method of collecting water. Its close proximity and lower level to the grave yard is worrying.

This well is dressed once a year, but this is a recent innovation. The dressings are held prior to those at Tissington, which had previously been recognised as the first in the year.

Hazelwood

The spring appropriately lies in Spring Hollow on the Farnah Green Road, at SK.334455. A good volume of water issues from it via a pipe, falling into a roadside gulley whence it flows via a culvert and thence to a nearby brook. A stone back secures the pipe, and the whole is shrouded by a stone portal which carries the inscription, 'Erected by Subscription in the 60th Year of H.M. Queen Victoria's Reign 1887'. Some locals can remember when this spring was used by the villagers of Hazelwood, who collected the water in milk churns.

Wormhill

The village spring was superceded by piped water many years ago. The spring still flows and feeds three troughs, one overflowing into the other, the last discharging into a gutter, thence to soak away in an adjoining field. Its attraction now is that it is a memorial to a son of the parish, the famous canal engineer James Brindley, who was born at nearby Tunstead within the parish of Wormhill.

The monument is a simple one, set amongst trees and shrubs, and adjoining the village stocks. It bears the legend '1875, in memory of James Brindley, Civil Engineer, Born in this Parish'. A further inscription has been added of later date, 'Important, this is not Drinking Water'. No doubt very good advice! This well is dressed on the last weekend in August, S.K.123743.

The Spring beneath St. John's Chapel, Artist's Corner, Matlock

A Spring under a Church

St. John's church at Matlock is a chapel of ease designed by Sir Guy Dawber, one of only a few designed by him. It is part of the parish of St. Giles at Matlock Old Town, and built in 1897. Built into the high retaining wall is a trough fed by a spring. The trough is large and is usually occupied by a frog. The spring can be heard running behind the trough even when there is insufficient water available to run out. This spring might be a lead mine sough, and the placing of this spring and trough in the foundations may be in deference to St. John the Baptist, S.K.295595.

A Genuine Roman Well

There are numerous claims in the county to 'Roman' remains; many of them are spurious, and one is inclined to believe that they are intended for the edification of tourists. We are inclined to forget that the Romans colonised us, and exerted an oppressive rule. Strange that we should wish them to take the credit for so much.

There is, or was, a genuine Roman well, which served the occupants of Little Chester or Derventio, now part of Derby. It was a military encampment of some importance. William Stukeley visited the site in 1721 and the plan he drew shows a well. He does not say if this is Roman or not, probably not so, for a contemporary house is indicated close by.

A stone lined well of certain Roman origin was found at the side of the present day Rykneld Street, Little Chester. Whilst a road linked Derventio to Aqua Arnametiae, and no doubt the people in the garrison travelled to Buxton for the baths, Little Chester too had its baths by the River Derwent, in a field called Parker's Piece, later the site of the playing fields for the Derby School. The Romans would have known about St. Alkmund's Well, but not by that name of course, not far distant, and itself close to Ryknield Street.

A Well in a Hotel

The Higham Farm Hotel boasts a well in its reception area. The well was 'lost' when it was filled in with rubbish shortly after the war, and was rediscovered in 1979.

It measures four feet (1.22m) diameter at the top and is 96ft (29.66m) deep including the water, which varies in depth but averages 20ft (6.1m). The bottom is bell shaped and an inscription in the wall of the well just above the bell and about half way down bears the date 1741.

The present owners of the hotel undertook considerable trouble in digging out the rubble and in restoring the well. The mouth is protected by a metal grid and a plate glass window. Floodlights have been installed, such that the visitor can now see down the well where the steening is clearly visible, as is the water at the bottom.

This was one of 23 wells listed in an inventory of wells in the parish dated 1885, when all but six were in use. Only three survive, the one referred to, one at Bull Farm (originally the Bull Inn, a famous visitor to which was Dick Turpin) and one at Well Farm. There is a Well Lane in the village, but the well has gone. It is said that when all the other wells in the village failed, the one at Higham Farm could be relied upon to supply the entire village with all its needs.

A Well that was Mined

Heath is an attractive village close to the M1 motorway, intersection 29. It once boasted a well in every garden. None of these are left, although stone troughs which were once used to hold the water can be seen in the village. The water stood on top of the Top Hard coal seam, which lies under the village rarely more than fifteen feet (4.6m) below the surface. Where this seam outcrops, springs occur, as in Sough Lane, or is it a sough? S.K.450664. The new maintenance depot for the motorway now covers the site of a medicinal spring which is lost forever. This water was used locally for eye troubles. A member of the Toft family from Heath, one-time village undertakers, boasted that a serious but unspecified eye condition was quickly cured by regular bathing in this spring.

Heath has dressed a well since 1976, but unfortunately it is an artificial 'mock up'. One well, near to the old smithy, now covered by a road widening scheme, was 'mined' for coal during the 1926 strike by a local collier and his family.

Roadside Drinking Places

The time was not so very long ago, that all road transport was by horse-drawn vehicles and riding was the only alternative to walking as a means of travelling. Pack-horse routes and later turnpike trusts established ways, many of which survive as thoroughfares today.

Apart from feeding and housing, the many horses and people need clean water to drink at frequent intervals. The springs in the county were exploited for this purpose wherever a stream was not available. There are numerous such watering places to be found, usually comprising a trough fed by a spring.

Some very nice examples can be found as follows, but beware, mostly the water to these is no longer clean enough for human consumption!

Littleover In the 'Hollow' a spring feeds two stone troughs now preserved by the local community. These make a very attractive feature, facing as they do one of the finest timber-framed houses in the county.

Brough This village is the site of Navio, a Roman settlement, mentioned elsewhere in connection with Bradwell's bath house. Opposite the Traveller's Rest (SK.184828) at the junction of the B6049 and A625 is a well. It is walled round, with a flight of steps descending to the water level. It was clearly designed to admit men only and not animals, so watering the latter must have been a laborious undertaking using buckets.

Troughs in Crich Market Place

on the old Ashbourne to Alfreton Turnpike

Clay Cross Waterworks Co. share certificate

courtesy of Cliff Williams

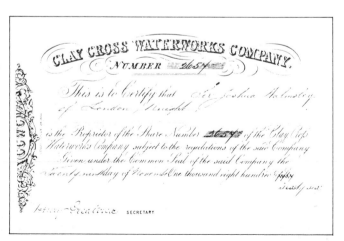

An Appeal

We take so much for granted in this country, and it is encouraging to see local pride taking an interest in our heritage. We are busily preserving buildings, engines, trams, mines and the like. Unfortunately our springs and wells, once so vital to our existence, are disappearing, witness the Becket Well in Derby, or are badly neglected, often the repository for rubbish. It is encouraging to hear of schemes for preserving these monuments, as for example Melbourne Civic Society's attempts to raise money to restore the Holy Well at Kings Newton.

The author appeals to local communities to take an interest in their local spring or well and to preserve and protect it from development, vandalism and the dumping of rubbish. It is surprising that some wells that are dressed with such splendour once a year, are neglected for the rest of the time. It would also be encouraging to see the resumption of some of the customs, such as Skak-bottle and Sugar-cupping. These traditions deserve preservation and could run in conjunction with the now well-established well dressings.

Acknowledgements

The author received considerable help from many people, but the following are thanked for their patience and help, and above all for their time and kindness.

Mr.A.ALLBEURY, Nestlé Co. Ltd.
Mr.W. BROOMHEAD, Pearson & Co. Ltd.
ANDREW KNIGHTON, Ilkeston
ADRIAN EARP, Melbourne
GRAHAM CUTTS, Whittington
GEORGE HAGUE, Hardwick Hall
Mrs. E.WHITE and ERNEST DUNKLEY, Bolsover Castle
Mr. M.TONG, Elvaston Castle
KITTY and ANDREW PORTER, Heath
Dr. LYNN WILLIES, Matlock Bath
ANDREW PUGH, Heights of Abraham Ltd.
THE BRITISH LEGION CLUB, Bakewell
GEORGE POWER, Belper Historical Society

I am indebted to the publishers, David Mitchell and George Power for their helpful suggestions, to the Institute of Geological Sciences for permission to quote freely from their publications, to the Borough of the High Peak for permission to quote the analysis of Buxton Water and to my wife and Marjorie Hunt for sharing my field visits in bad weather and correcting so many of my grammatical and spelling errors.

GAZETTEER of WELLS and SPRINGS

Alphabetically listed by name of nearest place

The absence of a grid reference suggests that the site is either lost or access is inadvisable.

	Place	Well	Page	Grid
A	Aldwark	Ducket Well*		229575
	Ashbourne	'water'	7	
	Ashleyhay	Folly well		294522
	Ashover*	Bath spring	46	344644
		Ashover House Hydro	52	
	Axe Edge	Dove Head spring	66	032685
B	Bakewell	Bath House spring*	30	218686
		Cappewell	28	lost
		Fountain	29	220687
		Great well	28	lost
		Growhill Lane spring		204692
		Peat well	30	293579
		St. Mary's well	28,30	lost
		Town well	29	lost
		Wicsop Wood spring	29	233684
	Barlow	Main well	22	
	Baslow	Lady well		257728
		Grand Hotel and Hydro	52	
	Belper	Lady well	23	
		Taylor well	31	
		Manor well	31	348465
	Birley Spa*		46	
	Bolsover	Conduit House spring	34	471708
	Bradwell	Bath House spring*	46	174820
	Brough	well*	74	184828
	Buxton	St. Anne's well*	22,39	057735
C	Castleton	Cave Dale spring	61	150826
		Russet well*	53,61	148828
		Speedwell level	61	139827
		Well of our Lady	24	148824
	Chapel en le frith	Nannys well		048808
	Chatsworth	Emperor spring	36	private
		Umberley spring	36	295704
		Umberley well	36	288696
	Chelmorton	Pippenwell		111692
		Five Wells*		123707
	Chesterfield	Holy Well	17	385711
		Market pump	17	385711
		Whittington Moor	8	386734
	Crich	troughs		350542
		Ridgeway sough	53	332549

	Place	Well or spring	Page	Grid
	Cromford	Alabaster sough	57	293570
		Bates sough	55	lost
		Cromford*	56	296569
		Dunsley spring*	63	268568
		Longhead sough	55	lost
		Roguelen spring	57	294562
		Vermuyden sough	55	lost
	Crowdecote	Crowdwell*		100653
D	Darley Dale	Clarke's Hydro	52	282622
		Hillcarr sough	60	259637
		Sharder well		286626
	Derby	Becket well	27	lost
		Roman well	72	private
		St. Alkmund's well*	15	352368
		Spa	46	lost
	Dimmingsdale	Hedess spring	26	172704
	Dove Dale	Nabs spring*		142537
E	Earl Sterndale	Dowel		076674
	Elvaston Castle	Coach House Wash pump	36	407330
		Kennel Cottage well	36	private
	Etwall	Town well	70	268319
	Eyam	Duric well		207782
		Hawkenedge well		215758
		Mompesson's well	69	223773
G	Glossop	Swineshaw springs	68	043958
	Great Hucklow			
	Grangemill	Shothouse spring*		242589
H	Hardwick Hall	Coal Yard	34	private
		St. Mary's well	33	462635
	Hartington	Lud well*		124624
	Hathersage	Little John's well		266795
		Robin Hood's well		269798
	Hazelwood	spring	71	334455
	Heath		73	
	Higham	Bull Farm well	73	private
		Higham Farm well	72	390590
		Well Farm well	73	private
	Howden Moor	(mostly in Yorkshire)		
		Bull Stones spring	68	179961
		Hoar Clough spring	68	145979
		Horse Shoe spring	68	162974
		Lord Edward Howard's spring	68	172964
		Lord Surrey's spring	68	184954
		Robin Hood's spring		193932
		Swains Greave	68	127975

	Place	Well or spring	Page	Grid
I	**Ible**	troughs		253569
	Ilkeston	Bath House*	46	lost
K	**Kedleston**	Bath House spring*	47	private
	Kings Newton	Holy Well	16	lost
	King Sterndale	Pictor spring		088722
		Thirst House Cave spring	25	097713
		Woo Dale spring		094725
L	**Little Hucklow**	Silver well	24	187803
	Littleover	troughs	74	330342
M	**Matlock**	Dimple Sough spring*	49	296604
		Chatsworth Hydro	51	305608
		Chesterfield House Hydro	51	
		Lillybank Hydro	51	303605
		Rockside Hydro	51	303609
		St. John's Church spring	72	295595
		Smedley's Hydro	50	300608
		Oldham House Hydro	51	
	Matlock Bath	Fountain Bath	44	294584
		Fountain Bath sough	44,54	294584
		Haliwell	17	lost
		Jacob's well	62	293586
		New Bath spring*	42	299579
		Old Bath spring*	42	lost
		Petrifying well	63	294582
		Royal well		293580
		Temple Hotel spring	44	293582
		Un-named thermal spring	45	294582
		Wragg sough	45	293583
	Melbourne	Chambers Row pump	31	lost
		Club Row pump	31	lost
		Hatton's well		
		(or Mary Ann Ince's pump)	33	
		Wash Pit	31	
		(or Lily Pool Spring)	31	388255
		Market Place pump	31	386253
		New York pump	31	lost
		Shaw's spring	31	lost
		Town pump	33	lost
	Monsal	Hob's Hurst Cave spring	26	175713
		Moss well		178723
	Monyash	Beresford's cutting		
		or Barsett's cut	58	172682
		Lathkil Head Cave	68	171659

	Place	Well or spring	Page	Grid
O	Over Haddon	Bubbling spring	58,68	205661
		Carter's Mill spring		182656
		Lathkill Dale sough	58	205661
		Mandale Mine	58	197661
P	Peak Forest	Adam's well		128796
		Cop well		129797
		Ebbing and Flowing Well		
		Barmoor clough	65	085797
Q	Quarndon	Chalybeate spring*	47	333407
R	Rowsley	Fallinge Edge spring		284674
S	Sheldon	Magpie sough	59	180696
	Shuttlewood	Thermal spring*	47	471734
	Smisby	Daniel Hay Farm	8	344207
	Stanton-by-Dale	Pump		465380
	Stoke	Stoke sough*	53	240764
	Stoney Middleton	Thermal spring*	47	232756
	Sudbury	Alder Moor Wood springs	36	
		Sudbury Coppice springs	36	157354
T	Taddington	High well*		144708
	Tideswell	Brook Head spring		141775
		Ebbing and Flowing well*	65	private
		Tor spring	23	141768
		Weeding well	66	
	Tissington	Coffin well	20	177522
		Hall well	20	176523
		Hands well	20	178523
		Town well*	20	175524
		Yew Tree well	20	174525
	Tutbury	Castle well	11	210302
W	West Hallam	Spa*	47	
	Wirksworth	Meerbrook sough	53,54	327552
		Wigwell		304544
		Thermal spring	48	lost
	Wormhill	Brindley spring	71	123743
		Wormhill springs*		124735
		Tunstead well*		109748
Y	Youlgreave	Bleakley Wood spring	38	217629
		Fountain	37	211643
		Mawstone spring	37	private

Those marked * are included in Farey's list of the 'notable springs of water in
Derbyshire'. There are many more in the list whose location is uncertain or lost.

Sources

Title	Author	Publisher	Date
Place Names of Derbyshire	Cameron	Cambridge	1959
Wells and Water Supply	Vince	Aylesbury	1978
Guide to Tutbury Castle	Somerville	Lancaster	1964
Citizen's Derby	Richardson	London	1949
History, Gazetteer and Directory of Derbys.	Bagshaw	Sheffield	1846
History of Melbourne	Briggs		1852
Melbourne	Jacques		1933
History of Chesterfield, Volume 1	Bestall	Chesterfield	1974
Thermal Springs, St. Annes's Well Buxton	Borough	Buxton	n.d.
John Smedley, 1803-1874, Centenary Exhibition	Charlton	Matlock	1974
The Beauty and Mystery of Well Dressing	Porteous	Derby	1949
Peak District Calendar of Events	Woodall	Private	n.d.
Derbyshire-Traditions	Daniel	Clapham	1975
Legends of Derbyshire	Merrill	Clapham	1975
Mysterious Derbyshire	Rickman/Nown	Clapham	1977
Caves of Derbyshire	ed. Ford	Clapham	1974
Lead Mining in the Peak District	ed. Ford/Rieuwerts	Bakewell	1975
The Caverns and Mines of Matlock Bath	Flindall/Hayes	Hartington	1976
Hardwick Hall	Girouard	N.T.	1976
Bolsover Castle	Faulkner	HMSO	1975
Youlgreave Water Works 1829-1979	Shimwell	Private	1979
Highways and Byeways in Derbyshire	Frith	London	1920
Bakewell, an Illustrated History	Allcock	Bakewell	1979
Strata of Derbyshire (1811)	Watson	Hartington	1973
Bulletin of the Peak District Mines Historical Society Vol. 7, Number 5	ed. Ford	Leicester	1980
Wells and Springs of Derbyshire	Stephens	I.G.S.	1929
Hydrogeochemistry of Groundwaters in the Derbyshire Dome	Edmunds	I.G.S.	1971
The Matlocks and their Past	Derbys, Cty. Lib.	Matlock	1977
The History of Shirland and Higham	Turbutt	Ogston	1978

Other books you may enjoy, published by **Scarthin Books** of Cromford: **Hanged for a Sheep:** *Crime in Bygone Derbyshire* by E.G.Power, Now in its second printing. **Journey from Darkness** by Gordon Ottewell, An adventure story for older Children, set in Victorian Derbyshire. Published Summer 1983: **The Peak District Quiz Book** by Barbara Hall. Do you really know the Peak? Over 300 questions set on 24 subjects, with a pictorial quiz, by the author of the 'Sheffield Quiz Book', and forthcoming: **Driving the Clay Cross Tunnel** by Cliff Williams. The hazardous work and rumbustious lives of railway navvies on the North Midland Line.